N R Rutter

26 October 1992

# Sketches at
# LORD'S

*Sketches at*
# LORD'S

*The Cricket Lithographs of John Corbet Anderson*

MICHAEL DOWN
DEREK WEST

*With a foreword by John Arlott*

WILLOW BOOKS
Collins
8 Grafton Street, London W1
1990

*To Hal and Eva Cohen*
*in gratitude and friendship*

Willow Books
William Collins Sons & Co Ltd
London · Glasgow · Sydney · Auckland
Toronto · Johannesburg

First published 1990
© Michael Down and Derek West and MCC 1990

BRITISH LIBRARY CATALOGUING IN PUBLICATION DATA
Down, Michael
Sketches at Lord's.
1. English lithographs. Anderson, John Corbet.
Special subjects. Cricket
I. Title   II. West, Derek   III. Anderson, John Corbet
769.92′4

ISBN 0-00-218342-0

Set in Linotron Sabon by
Rowland Phototypesetting Ltd,
Bury St Edmunds, Suffolk
Originated, printed and bound by C.S. Graphics Pte Ltd Singapore

*Frontispiece: John Corbet Anderson.*
*In the garden of his Croydon home the year before his death.*

# Contents

# Foreword

The lithographs of John Corbet Anderson are the products of a very narrow time period in British popular art. They were produced in the middle of the nineteenth century when picture production in this country had passed out of the phase of aquatint and before it moved into photography. Aquatinting demanded a degree of workmanship – perhaps one should say processes of workmanship – more complicated than lithography but, of course, far simpler than photography.

This was also the period when cricket evolved from a rustic pursuit into a popular one. Indeed, it assumed the trappings of seniority and became the first demandingly skilful team game. W. G. Grace was about to give the game a standing of Victorian respectability, but of course he came too late for Anderson and the popular lithographers. Alas! What a splendid subject he would have made.

The setting of Anderson's work is historically important, but above all its artistic quality is considerable. In the first place, it was generally agreed that he invariably achieved a good likeness, which may seem a simple point in these days of photography but, in fact, it was extremely important at that time. His work was also sensitive and imaginative. Technically, in the development of lithography it came after the early, somewhat scratchy days and before the aesthetically unpleasing chromolithography. Uncoloured, his work has the most desirable pencil-chalk quality; the coloured versions are delicate and completely pleasing. From the start, too, Corbet Anderson ensured that the technical processes by which they were reproduced were of the highest quality. There was no better early lithographic process than that of Hullmandel, and the standard was maintained throughout.

It is most important, however, as Messrs Down and West point out, that while the title 'Sketches at Lord's' was carried by much of the best of Anderson's work, it was such an obvious selling point that it was pirated. It was stolen by Mourilyan and Casey and used on work of inferior quality which, in its turn, had also been stolen – from Basébe's earlier engravings.

At the other extreme, while the portrait of Alfred Mynn is probably the best known of Anderson's portraits, that of Joseph Guy is extremely well executed and subtle in feeling. Above all, the United All England XI is a very fine composite lithograph indeed. It is not of any eleven that actually took the field but a collection of eleven outstanding players of the period, all first undertaken as separate portraits. This is Anderson at his best. He was not a cricketer, or at least, cricket was by no means his major interest, and these are essentially portraits of men who happen to be cricketers. It may be observed, too, that he captures character most artfully in, for instance, his portrait of Charles Brown of Nottingham. In fact it is probably significant that the series of cricketing 'attitudes' is the least satisfying of his series.

Anderson was, on the other hand, something of an antiquarian, historian, and student of ecclesiastical matters. This most certainly accounts for the variety of items in the backgrounds to his portraits – tents, windmills, churches, but rarely cricket scenes.

In their time, Anderson's lithographs were respected rather than cheaply popular. Later, of course, they suffered doubly: first from the immense public response to the sale of photographs, and then from the arrival on the scene of a fresh generation of cricket heroes. That must largely account for the fact that so many of them must have been discarded – which is the reason for their scarcity today. They were virtually eclipsed in public esteem until relatively recent years, and in a way they enjoyed an unexpected growth in popularity. The sale of Colonel Sloane-Stanley's collection probably did more than anything else to summon the work out of obscurity. Certainly, a few years before the last war it was possible to buy them for shillings, where they would now cost hundreds of pounds.

In the field of cricket literature there had, of course, been John Nyren's *The Young Cricketer's Tutor* and *The Cricketers of My Time* – both edited by Charles Cowden Clarke – relatively early in the century, but nothing else to equal in literary merit the artistic quality of Anderson's work. The standard of cricket reporting was pedestrian and unimaginative. It was not until the twentieth century that cricket writing attained a literary quality that could be even remotely compared with that of Nyren–Clarke.

For all these reasons, the cricket lithographs of John Corbet Anderson stand virtually alone in an island of time and artistry.

JOHN ARLOTT
*Alderney*

# *Preface*

Over recent years there has been something of a boom in the collecting of cricket art and memorabilia. Cricket, always a game of nostalgia, is now the subject of regular specialized auctions which attract an increasing array of collectors and dealers. This development reached a peak with the much-publicized Bicentenary Sale held by the MCC in 1987, when collectors from all over the world bid furiously for a mouth-watering display of cricket treasures.

Among the most desirable and attractive of these collectors' items is a well-known but increasingly rare series of mid-Victorian lithographic portraits drawn by John Corbet Anderson. Coming just before the introduction of photography, these lithographs provide the only pictorial record of many famous cricketing names from one of the game's most romantic eras. As well as demonstrating a high degree of artistic ability, they are charmingly evocative of a bygone era. The Anderson series has been described by John Arlott as the 'pinnacle of popular cricket art'.

Despite the undoubted quality and collectability of these prints, the full extent of the series has never before been properly understood. Even less has been known of the Scottish antiquary John Corbet Anderson, who produced the pictures. A handful of the prints have been reproduced in other cricket books, but many are virtually unknown and no proper listing has ever appeared. This book, which takes its title from Anderson's 'Sketches at Lord's' series, is intended to fill this undoubted gap and will hopefully introduce many more people to both the pictures and the players of an era which saw the birth of the modern game.

Much painstaking research has gone into the compiling of a definitive catalogue of the lithographs. The entire series of over fifty different prints is reproduced, along with previously unknown publication details and biographies of the players who are depicted. These biographies have been assembled over a number of years from a variety of sources in order to give an added dimension to the portraits.

It is almost ten years since we discovered a mutual fascination with the Anderson lithographs. Over that period every new discovery and piece in the jigsaw has been exchanged and discussed until the story was clear enough to deserve publication. Although the book is a joint effort in every way, the sternest reviewers can direct any blame to GDW for the biographies of the players and the section on Cricket's Middle Ages, and to MGD for details of the lithographs and the rest of the text.

Finally, a special vote of thanks to our respective wives, Margaret Down and Mary West, for their assistance, sympathy and patient understanding throughout our quest for John Corbet Anderson.

MICHAEL DOWN                    DEREK WEST
*Holmes Chapel*                     *Caversham*

# *Acknowledgements*

The authors and publishers would like to thank the following for their generous assistance in a wide variety of ways:

Irene Allardice, David Rayvern Allen, David Anstice, John Arlott, E. K. 'Ted' Brown, John Claughton (Eton College), J. R. Clube, Hal and Eva Cohen, Michael Doggart, Major Ian Dyer, John Gill, Paul Goldman (Department of Prints and Drawings, British Museum), Judith Gordon, W. L. Gray (Curator, Melbourne Cricket Club Museum), Stephen Green (Curator and Librarian of the MCC who has been associated with this book from its beginning), Diana Rait Kerr, John McKenzie, Robin Marlar, A. O. Meakin and his staff at the Croydon Central Library, Miss R. de B. Monk (Parker Gallery), Rupert Neelands (Christie's), Nottinghamshire County Library, Nick Potter (Burlington Gallery), David Ridge, Romford Central Library, Stephen Saunders, Paul Sowan/Muriel Shaw (Croydon Natural History and Scientific Society), Patricia Towns, Y. M. Walker, Tony Winder and Peter Wynne-Thomas (Curator and Librarian at Trent Bridge).

# Introduction

## Cricket Art

The term 'cricket picture' covers a vast range of illustrative material connected with the game – from classical eighteenth-century oils of children holding a cricket bat to the most humble cigarette card or photograph. Collectors of such pictures are often far from discriminating – anything related to cricket is fair game. Indeed, this tendency has led to even the most famous of collections containing some material of both doubtful provenance and dubious artistic quality. Within this vast assemblage of illustrative material – and it has been produced continuously for some 250 years – the portrait work of Anderson must surely stand near the top of the tree among 'pure' cricket pictures.

The history of the cricket picture has been best documented by John Arlott in a number of books (see Bibliography). He has noted that until the early Victorian years, when the engravings and lithographs of Watts, Felix, Basébe, Drummond and Anderson appeared, there had been little that qualified as true cricket art. Only the early depictions of cricket matches by Boitard and Hayman, and their derivatives in the form of broadsheets and book illustrations, come readily to mind. For the rest, the early cricket pictures were mainly either fashionable portraits with cricket items as props, or topographical views including a cricket match as an incidental feature. Around the 1840s and 1850s, however, cricket underwent a transformation in popularity. There were many factors at work. The early Victorians began to imbue the old gambling game with a new respectability; first roundarm and later overarm bowling transformed the technique of the game; and the touring elevens carried the gospel to all parts of the country on the newly invented railway system. With this surge in popularity and the dramatic improvement in communications, the first real sporting heroes of Britain were created – Mynn, Lillywhite, Pilch, Box, Hillyer, Parr and a host of others. Once the public began to take an interest in these players as individuals, they naturally created a demand to see them in pictures.

With photography still just around the corner, it was the illustrative medium of the day – lithography – which enabled portrait likenesses of these players to be sold to a large and admiring public. With only a very few isolated exceptions these were the first portraits of famous cricketers to appear. But for Anderson, and to a lesser extent Felix, Basébe and Drummond, we would have no pictorial record of these great cricketers from the era that essentially led to the birth of the modern game.

The earliest true cricketing lithographs in this mid-nineteenth-century heyday were the series of five by G. F. Watts depicting various batting strokes. These are arguably the finest of all cricket images, but, although probably modelled on Felix, they were not intended as portraits of actual players. Later Watts produced two more 'action' lithographs, but this time the identities were clear – Alfred Mynn and Fuller Pilch.

Shortly afterwards, in the 1840s, Charles Basébe and William Drummond produced a number of paintings of famous cricketers which were reproduced by the finest engravers of the day. Nicholas Wanostrocht ('Felix') also painted a number of sensitive studies of himself and his fellow cricketers around this time. Several of these were lithographed (although not by Felix's own hand), most notably his magnificent group painting of the All England Eleven.

The demand for such pictures was being clearly demonstrated. Other memorabilia of the players were also coming on to the market, and the famous Staffordshire figures of the cricketers Parr and Caesar date from this period. It was also an era which saw players and ex-players able to make a living out of the game. William Clarke instituted and managed the touring All England Eleven; various players opened sports-goods businesses or shops; others leased and operated cricket grounds. Soon there were to be the first overseas tours. Into this fertile environment stepped one of cricket's first publishing entrepreneurs – Fred Lillywhite. His fascinating story is told elsewhere in this book, but for the moment we should note that it was he who took on board the young artist John Corbet Anderson and produced a series of popular cricketing portraits of unprecedented scope – Lillywhite published the pictures and sold, reviewed and advertised them unstintingly.

What are the reasons behind the lasting appeal of these pictures? They were not produced at the time as 'art' but as popular illustrations to be hawked around the cricket grounds in the same way as postcard photographs or magazines might be today. The answer is perhaps to be found not only in their pleasing and evocative appearance, but also in the manner of their production. Here, *production* is the key word. So much that we refer to as 'a cricket print' is merely *re*production by any one of dozens of essentially photographic processes – for example the reproductions in this book. The true lithograph can rightly be described as 'original art' despite the fact that many hundreds of copies of each may have been printed.

It was Anderson's skill which went into every stage of the production of these prints, so they are just as much originals as a painting or drawing. As well as sketching the subject, Anderson also transposed the image on to stone.

*This Staffordshire figure is traditionally believed to represent*
*Julius Caesar, here shown in Anderson's original sketch.*

He probably also supervised while an expert craftsman printed each copy individually, right down to the final hand colouring if it were required. Few cricket prints, aside from the lithographs, can claim this tag of 'original art', most being merely interpretations and repetitions of drawings or paintings by artists who were often themselves of only moderate accomplishment. They lack the spark of genius and the hallmark of originality that characterize the work of Anderson and, to an even greater extent, Watts.

The best of the Andersons have a marvellous depth and character about them. Coupled, as in this volume, with a knowledge of the player's life and career, the lithographs portray the individual's personality to a remarkable degree – the study of Alfred Mynn is a perfect example which tells more than any photograph could ever have done.

When Anderson tried to imitate Watts' 'action' studies he clearly failed, but as a portrait artist he was truly the 'photographer of his age'. Arthur Haygarth, the compiler of *Scores and Biographies*, frequently stated how closely the portraits resembled their subjects. These opinions, though somewhat repetitious, are quoted in many of the biographical notices as a reliable guide to authenticity as well as to Anderson's artistic merit, since Haygarth, a first-class cricketer himself, was well acquainted with the players of the period.

In a field of art which has not always been of the highest standard, this impressive body of work surely stands out as a unique record of part of Britain's sporting heritage.

# Cricket's Middle Ages – The 1850s

In the decade before the issue of John Corbet Anderson's lithographs, cricket began to experience a development that would transform it from a largely local pastime into a national sport. Various factors contributed to this process of evolution. Public interest was stimulated by the editorial policy of *Bell's Life*, the principal sporting newspaper of the time, which whetted the appetite of its eager readers with an extensive coverage of the game, thanks to postal reforms facilitating the cheap and rapid transmission of match reports. The number of playing fields throughout the country was augmented, particularly in garrison towns in accordance with the Army's policy of providing soldiers with sporting amenities. Finally, and possibly the most important factor of all, there was the incalculable improvement in transport created by the construction of the railways, rendering obsolescent in many areas the more precarious journeys by stage-coach.

All these factors combined to produce a unifying influence which was not, however, to be realized for some years to come. In a state of transition at the period of Anderson's portraits, cricket was markedly dissimilar from the more highly organized game of the late twentieth century. Although a few of the counties, chiefly those in the south, used to play against each other at times, there was no official county championship nor any limited-overs competition. Single-wicket contests still retained some popularity, and the superior status of a few genuine 'grand matches', such as Gentlemen *v* Players and occasional encounters between North and South, was admitted, but the more modern rigid distinction between first-class and other cricket was not so apparent. There were no Test matches until 1876–77, but the inaugural tour abroad (not first-class) took place in 1859, when a party of twelve professionals – nine of whom are featured in Anderson's portraits – made a brief visit to Canada and the USA.

The growing interest in cricket created circumstances favourable to the birth of a new institution destined to give an enormous fillip to the proliferation of the game – the Itinerant Eleven, of which there were several. First and most famous was the All England Eleven (AEE), founded in 1846 by William Clarke, a shrewd speculator and superb lob bowler from Nottingham. In return for satisfactory financial arrangements Clarke was willing to take his team, consisting mainly of the best professionals of the day, to play against local sides in any part of the country. The idea caught on, and soon the AEE became a thriving concern, boosting the public demand for more cricket at all levels. In 1852 a rival body, the United All England Eleven (UAEE), was established by John Wisden and James Dean, who attracted to their team those professionals unable to get on with Clarke and his methods. After Clarke's death, the 'Two Elevens' met in a series of benefit matches (1857–69) often regarded as the premier fixtures of the season. A further rift occurred in 1864, causing a schism between North and South, and the southern professionals abandoned their old allegiances to form a new organization called the United South of England Eleven (USEE). Many of the cricketers portrayed by Anderson played for at least one of the Itinerant Elevens.

The AEE and its imitators were rarely engaged in first-class contests. Most of their matches were played against 'odds', with the local sides fielding as many as twenty-two men. As an additional measure to offset the superiority of the AEE, the home teams were often strengthened by the temporary engagement of one or more professionals, known as 'Given Men'.

A cricketer of today would scarcely relish the prospect of batting against 'odds', striving vainly to pierce the mob of opposing fielders. Equally, he would be nonplussed and in some instances appalled by the conditions familiar to the players of the 1850s. The attention lavished on the preparation of grounds today was unheard of in J. C. Anderson's time. Pitches were uneven, well grassed, and dangerous to life and limb – Lord's was particularly notorious in this respect – and the outfield was occasionally unshorn. Overs consisted of four balls, most of the bowlers employing the round-arm delivery (over-arm was not permitted until 1864), though there were still a few lob bowlers to be found. Sightscreens had not been invented, and there were few boundaries: at Lord's, four runs were awarded for a ball striking the Pavilion, but otherwise all hits had to be run out. The combination of exhaustion brought on by so much running and the necessity of coping with a constant stream of shooters and bouncers told heavily against the batsmen, even though some of the bowlers described as 'fast' would probably have been nearer medium-fast by twentieth-century standards. Consequently, a good defence was much admired, criticism of slow batting was far more muted than it is today, individual scores reaching double figures were considered worthy of comment, and batting averages of 20 or more were lauded as 'enormous'.

Some of the names of the fielding positions have altered since the 1850s. 'Middle wicket', stationed at either the on or the off side, was the equivalent of mid-on or mid-off. First slip was known as 'short slip', sometimes supported by 'long slip' (close third man) and 'cover slip' (second slip). Of the two specialist posts in the field, one is now not common (point), the other a mere memory (long-stop).

Apart from a slight suggestion of 'Sunday best', Anderson's portraits provide a good record of cricket costume and equipment in the 1850s. It is known that the collars and ties worn by many of his subjects were often removed during the actual course of play, while coloured shirts or patterns with spots or stripes were commonly preferred to those in plain white. The top hats of the early prints, so beloved in popular imagination, are shown as yielding before 1860 to the more functional caps. Similarly, the white flannel trousers, no longer supported by braces, are maintained in position by an adjustable waistband at the back, sometimes reinforced by a belt. Different patterns of footwear are illustrated, some white, some brown or black, some consisting of alternating dark and light strips. The all-white model was not universally adopted until many years after the period of Anderson's lithographs. Spliced handles for bats were just coming into use, and the blades, when viewed in profile, were flatter than those of today. The few examples of protective gear illustrated include different types of leg-guards and the gloves worn by batsmen and wicket-keepers.

---

⁓

---

# The Men Behind
# the Pictures

## The Artist:
## John Corbet Anderson

Within the specialist world of early cricket pictures the name J. C. Anderson is revered solely for the series of evocative and accurate cricketing lithographs that bear his name. Few of those enthusiasts who seek his work so avidly in the sale rooms and galleries are aware of any personal details behind the familiar phrase 'John Corbet Anderson del et lith'. Was he a famous artist or a talented amateur? His cricket portraits have survived for over 130 years and are now more popular than ever, but what else did he achieve?

John Corbet Anderson, although of Scottish ancestry, was born in London on 17 January 1827. His father, Dr William Anderson, was a naval surgeon formerly with the East India Company, and his mother Marion was a member of the well-known Shropshire family of Corbet. Young John, the second son, was brought up in conventional Victorian middle-class surroundings. The family was neither poor nor wealthy, and there was strict adherence to religious and moral values. A modest private education was arranged in the Andersons' native Scotland, at Rothesay on the Isle of Bute, but this was cut short at the age of fifteen when John was sent to an attorney's office to study law. After just three weeks the youthful Anderson showed his first signs of a strong will by declaring that the legal profession would never be appropriate for him. As a child he had shown considerable gifts of painting and drawing, and it was art that filled his thoughts rather than the daily grind of a solicitor's office.

Luckily, at this moment of family crisis young John's uncle was able to introduce him to the famous artist Benjamin Robert Haydon. Haydon was impressed by the youngster's potential and promptly agreed to take him on as a pupil and assistant. From the first the relationship proved fruitful, and the impressionable Anderson devoted himself to emulating his new mentor. With regard to artistic skills, this could not have been more beneficial. At the age of sixteen Anderson had a life-size cartoon – 'The Plague of London – 1665' – chosen in a prize competition as one of the designs to be used in the decoration of the new Houses of Parliament. His career seemed to be set fair to follow in his mentor's footsteps.

Haydon was a gifted artist and a well-known figure, but he was on a tragic path. In 1846, with Anderson barely nineteen years old, Haydon committed suicide, in a desperate mixture of frustrated talent and misplaced ideals. His huge and grandiose paintings had achieved a certain acclaim, but were a financial disaster (he was imprisoned for debt on several occasions). He was a turbulent and quarrelsome character who often alienated his clients and antagonized the Academy. He tried endless schemes for promoting his reputation as an artist and for making money, but in all these he ultimately failed. The Houses of Parliament competition in which Anderson won a prize was a case in point. Haydon had petitioned for such a scheme for over thirty years, and when the authorities finally took up the idea he threw all his energies into his own entry. Alas, it was rejected by the judges. An attempted solo exhibition shortly afterwards also ended in failure, and this contributed to his suicide.

Haydon's death was a crushing shock to the impressionable Anderson and served to arrest the pupil's promising artistic career. For a few years he earned a tolerable living as a portrait painter in Liverpool, but he soon decided to pursue his interests in history and writing rather than stay exclusively with art. It was during this period in Liverpool, however, that he embarked upon his series of cricketing portraits – the earliest and probably the best being executed when he was still only twenty-three years of age. Since Anderson was to remain a full-time professional artist for only some five years, it was the happiest twist of fate which led him to produce a body of work which has endured and given pleasure for so many years.

By 1852, despite the popularity of the 'Sketches at Lord's' series, Corbet Anderson had decided to pursue a career as historian and writer. His first great self-appointed task was to be a study of the historic parish church at Croydon, and he duly moved in with his sisters at Duppas Hill. This started an association with Croydon that was to remain unbroken until his death more than fifty years later. For the first three of those years, with the initial batch of cricket portraits behind him, Anderson laboured diligently and ceaselessly on tracing the history of the church and in illustrating its most pleasing features. In 1855 he produced his first book, published privately through subscription and titled *Monuments and Antiquities of Croydon Church*. Although containing only twenty pages of text, the eleven folio-sized plates were masterpieces of patient labour and meticulous precision. Barely twelve years later the church was completely destroyed by fire, and it was

*An example of Anderson's non-cricket works,*
*his beloved Croydon Church.*

only through Anderson's illustrations that many of the historic monuments could be rebuilt or restored. Over the years he published two more books concerning the church; these provided a magnificent historical record and were a testimony to his skill, but of course, they could hardly produce much of an income. The subscription list for these beautifully produced epics numbered barely 200, and this hardly covered the costs of production.

After this first literary achievement there followed more activity on the cricket lithographs, presumably as a means of providing income for the less commercial projects that lay ahead. During subsequent years Anderson steeped himself in local history and truly earned his title of 'The Historian of Croydon'. A series of works on the parish was issued and brought together as *Chronicles of Croydon* in the 1870s, again with his own illustrations enhancing the text. Other books followed at regular intervals, and these are listed in the Bibliography. Always, though, there was a long period of painstaking research before his findings were committed to print.

Year after year was spent poring over obscure documents, and the British Museum Reading Room became almost a second home; at the time of his death he was the longest-serving holder of a Reader's Ticket – sixty years. How the family finances withstood this existence is hard to understand, but, true to the spirit of Haydon, his researches had to come first. The subject matter – local history, archaeology, religion – may appear rather dull to modern eyes, but the scholarship and dedication are unmistakable, and always there are the precise illustrations – lithographs, woodcuts and steel engravings.

Aside from his work, Corbet Anderson's private life followed this same pattern of sober, Christian values. He raised six sons and a daughter, and despite his introspective nature was a well-known local figure. He lectured on historical matters, showed visitors around the parish, and was active in local politics, particularly with regard to the incorporation of Croydon as a Parliamentary Borough. He maintained a close association with the parish church and was one of the leading bell-ringers. On Sundays he could often be found in the poorer areas of Croydon attempting to convert the non-churchgoers.

His family's life was necessarily rather spartan, since financial gain never figured prominently in Anderson's obscure literary tasks. One contemporary described him as 'always struggling, poorly recompensed . . . barred from the fellowship of learned societies by chronic impecuniosity'. In 1896 he endeavoured to raise some money by selling his modest collection of archaeological items – Roman coins, medieval pots etc. – most of which had been given to him over the years by friends and colleagues in local history circles. By today's materialistic standards Anderson might seem somewhat self-indulgent. Family finances were looking particularly grim at one stage when he was fortunate enough to receive a commission from a local dignitary, Joseph Leete, to investigate that gentleman's family history. This arduous labour occupied the last twenty years of Corbet Anderson's life and enabled him and his wife to maintain basic home comforts and peace of mind. Happily, he lived just long enough to see the mighty task published.

Anderson was very much a Victorian, not only in era but also in character. He valued the basic Christian standards of family, hard work and austerity. His personality is described by contemporaries in such phrases as 'solitary thinker', 'deep nature', 'lofty purity of morals' and 'modest and retiring'. He was quite simply a thorough scholar and a talented artist.

Despite living until his eightieth year, Anderson never enjoyed robust health and his end came through a chill caught while waiting to address the Selborne Society in his beloved Croydon parish church. He refused to stop work, and soon died 'in harness' at his desk. His was a life dedicated to scholarship and art, played out to a small audience but leaving behind works of permanence and value – a legacy far greater than mere wealth.

# *The Printers*

Almost all of the Anderson lithographs indicate the name of the printer as well as the artist and publisher. This is seldom the practice on aquatints or engravings, for the simple reason that the skill of the printer in these processes is less critical than in the production of good-quality lithographs. From the point of view of cataloguing and identifying Anderson's works the name of the printer is invaluable information, but we shall see that it also has a bearing on the artistic quality of the lithograph. Before discussing the various printers who produced Anderson's prints, it would be helpful to look briefly at the lithographic technique and the history of its development.

The common print-making techniques can be divided into three main processes: relief, intaglio and planographic. The common names associated with these processes include:

Relief – woodcut, wood engraving, linocut

Intaglio – line engraving (copper or steel), aquatint, mezzotint, etching, stipple engraving, dryprint, soft-ground etching

Planographic – lithograph

Relief and intaglio processes both involve cutting or incising a pattern or design into a plate, coating it with ink and then printing on to paper using a press. The essential difference between them is that in relief processes the area *not* to be printed is cut away, whereas the opposite applies for intaglio.

The planographic (or lithographic) technique is, however, quite different. As its name implies, the print is made directly from what is drawn on a flat surface and there is no cutting or engraving involved. The process is based on the fact that grease repels water. The design is first drawn on a block of limestone with tusche or crayon containing grease. The stone is then etched and washed with turpentine to remove the soap and wax from the crayon or tusche. In order to print, the stone is first dampened and then inked, the drawing on the stone repelling the water, and the film of water on the bare parts repelling the ink. Therefore only those parts of the stone that have been drawn on receive the ink. Paper is laid on the stone in a flat-bed press, and the design is transferred. In this way thousands of prints can be made from one stone.

Since a single stone can only properly be used to print a single colour, greater texture and depth can be added to the picture by subsequent use of a second stone (called a tintstone) inked with a pale buff wash. (The use of a tintstone often results in a small pinprick visible in the lower corner of the lithograph which is used to keep the two stones in register, and this can be seen on many of the Anderson prints.) Lithographs in multiple colours can be made by printing with coloured inks, using a separate stone for each colour. But more often, as in the case of the Anderson lithographs, colour was simply added by hand.

In fact the printing process is highly complicated, and the skill of the lithographic printer is a vital component in the production. A knowledge of chemistry is needed for the etching and degreasing operations; different artistic effects require different degrees of acid etch, and a special combination of artistic appreciation and scientific understanding is therefore required. During printing, the skilled printer might interrupt the operation to make corrections with razor blade, acid solution and ink.

The basic principles of this complex process were invented by a German, Aloys Senefelder, in 1798. This constituted the first important development in print-making for centuries. Senefelder's aim was to develop a cheap, commercial process for reproducing drawings. His method was quickly taken up by artists, particularly in France where Delacroix and Daumier lent the new technique respectability.

The earliest Anderson lithographs were printed by the firm of Hullmandel and Walton. In choosing this printer from the hundreds then available, Anderson had gone to the most respected name in the business. Charles Joseph Hullmandel had been by far the leading figure in the early development and introduction of the new lithographic techniques in Britain. Born in 1789 in Mayfair, of a French mother and German father, Hullmandel was a competent artist in his own right, having trained in Paris. During a sketching holiday in Germany in 1817 he had met Senefelder and learned the secrets of the new print-making process. On his return to Britain he immediately adopted the technique in order to publish his '24 Views of Italy, drawn from nature and engraved on stone by Charles Hullmandel'. This was really the first series of topographical lithographs to be published in Britain. Unfortunately the work suffered from the very amateurish printing by the firm Moser and Harris.

This experience inspired Hullmandel to learn everything he could about the lithographic process. He started his own printing press at his home in 1819 and he even studied chemistry under the great Michael Faraday in order to perfect the complex printer's art. Over the next thirty years Hullmandel was responsible for nearly all the significant developments in the technique of lithography. He is credited with improvements via the use of graduated tints and white in the highlights. Much of this was published in patents and in his classic book *The Art of Drawing on Stone*, first published in 1824.

More than anybody else Hullmandel was responsible for the success of topographical lithography – he produced over 150 different books of such prints – during the period when the new technique ousted the aquatint as the pre-eminent method of reproduction. He was a commercial printer, but he attracted all the leading artists because of the combination he provided. His technical mastery of the process, allied to the fact that he had started out as an accomplished artist/draughtsman, made him a great printer.

In 1843 Hullmandel formed the company of Hullmandel and Walton. His partner was almost certainly J. F. Walton, and not the leading artist and lithographer W. L. Walton who was responsible for 'The View of Tonbridge School' and several other cricketing prints. During the 1840s, while Hullmandel and Walton's work was of the highest standard, they were overtaken in terms of volume of business by the firm of Day and Haghe (later Day and Sons, and then Vincent Brooks, Day and Son), and by 1850 this company had taken over the mantle of the leading litho press. There were also other notable printers at the time, such as C. Graf, the Hanharts, Ducote, Dickinson and others. Although Charles Hullmandel died in 1850, the firm of Hullmandel and Walton continued to operate for a number of years. By now, however, the lithographic technique was well established and printers had sprung up all over the country. This proved to be the peak, however, as the invention of photography was soon to revolutionize the graphic arts.

Returning to the Anderson prints, one can see from the Catalogue that three different printers were used. The abbreviation 'del et lith' indicates, however, that in every case Anderson himself not only drew the original picture from life but also translated it on to the stone. Nevertheless, he always entrusted the actual printing to a specialist. The first series of pictures in 1850 and 1851 was printed by the firm of Hullmandel and Walton, and although Hullmandel himself was dead by that time, the quality is still high.

In 1852–53 the printing transferred to Richard Black, and we can assume that the unattributed 'Sketches at Lord's' series was also by this printer. Despite being Anderson's most famous and oft-encountered work, the quality on these is not as good as the earlier prints. Whether this is the fault of the printer, the artist or the greater difficulty in lithographing smaller designs is hard to say. Little is known of Black other than that he operated his printing press in Fleet Street, but he was certainly not one of the leading printers of the day. Neither was the firm that took over for the last series of lithographs between 1855 and 1860 – Stannard and Dixon. By this time Fred Lillywhite was firmly in charge of the commercial side of Anderson's work and he doubtless arranged for a less expensive firm of printers. Nevertheless, Stannard and Dixon successfully produced many popular forms of illustration, including a number of music and song covers.

In all probability the subsequent hand colouring of the lithographs was also done by the printer. This was certainly carried out to the artist's precise specifications, however, as evidenced by one surviving copy of the tinted Alfred Diver print which has colouring instructions in the margin in Anderson's unmistakable handwriting.

# *The Publishers*

At various times there were four people involved in the publication of the Anderson lithographs – Robert Dark, Frederick Lillywhite, John Wisden and Anderson himself. Between the years 1850 and 1860 the combination of these individuals changed in the following sequence:

1 Anderson and Dark
2 Anderson and Lillywhite
3 Lillywhite and Wisden
4 Lillywhite alone

The reasons for these changes are described in the following chapter (see page 27 *et seq.*).

The earliest prints were published by Anderson in conjunction with Robert Dark, whose place of business was in the Lord's Ground itself. Dark was the youngest of three brothers, the eldest being James Henry Dark, the proprietor of Lord's for almost thirty years from 1835. The brothers were from the humblest of family backgrounds, but all turned out to be successful businessmen: James made a considerable success out of running Lord's, and the other two, Robert and Benjamin, were cricket equipment manufacturers.

Benjamin concentrated on selling bats and balls, whereas Robert was a glove, leg-guard and ball maker. He had been apprenticed to John Small (Senior) of Hambledon fame and eventually bought the old man's cricket ball-making tools shortly before Small died in 1829. Not long after this brother Benjamin also died, and Robert took over the entire family ball business. There was always a great rivalry with the famous firm of Duke & Sons but, as one might expect, Dark had a monopoly on the supply of balls for the 'Great' matches at Lord's, and he played this advantage to the hilt.

As well as ball making, Robert Dark credited himself as sole inventor of 'Tubular India Rubber Gloves' and 'Improved Leg Guards'. He ran the business successfully until his death in 1873 at the age of seventy-one. He was always a familiar figure at Lord's and for many years also acted as money-taker on the gate. Clearly the Darks liked to keep everything within the family, so it is hardly a surprise that when Robert joined young Corbet Anderson in the publication of cricket portraits it was his elder brother, James, who became the first subject. It was surely only family loyalty that caused the proprietor of Lord's to be chosen before such playing heroes as Alfred Mynn and Fuller Pilch.

We do not know the financial arrangements of this initial publishing partnership of Anderson and Dark, but the latter's principal contribution was probably to provide an outlet at Lord's Ground for selling the pictures. This association continued into the second year of publication, but the success of the venture had already attracted the attention of a young man from a famous cricketing family – Frederick Lillywhite.

Frederick was the son of the great William Lillywhite who had pioneered the introduction of round-arm bowling. Unlike his brothers John and James, Frederick had no great aptitude for playing cricket, but during his short life he

*Fred Lillywhite, a pioneer in many cricketing ventures and the business brain behind Anderson's lithographs.*

made quite a reputation in any number of business ventures associated with the game.

From an early age he displayed tremendous energy as an entrepreneur. In 1848, at the age of nineteen, he introduced his portable printing press to the cricket grounds of England. He travelled to all the big matches producing up-to-the-minute scorecards, a service he was to continue until his death. Each evening he would also post to subscribers the details of the day's play. This remarkable service meant that for an annual cost of £2 a subscriber could receive a scoresheet of the previous day's play almost every morning during the summer. At the same time the young Lillywhite was also acting as reporter on the major matches for the weekly sporting newspaper *Bell's Life*.

From 1848 until his death in 1866, Fred Lillywhite was continuously coming up with new schemes connected with cricket. Throughout this period he produced his *Guide to Cricketers*, the most important cricket annual to appear before *Wisden's Almanack*. He also undertook a variety of other publishing ventures, the first (1853) being Arthur Haygarth's compilation of *Public School Matches* which ran through many editions. In 1859 he organized and accompanied the first overseas tour (George Parr's team to Canada and the USA). On his return from this perilous undertaking he wrote and published the first Tour Book, a memorable and readable account of the team's journeys – which were undertaken complete with Lillywhite's printing tent and associated paraphernalia.

In 1862 he produced the first four volumes of *Scores and Biographies*, the massive result of Arthur Haygarth's lifelong labours. This had become one of Lillywhite's grand ambitions, and he threw all his considerable energies into the project over a number of years. As if all this activity were not enough, he maintained a sports outfitters and general cricket supplies business, in one form or another, throughout his working life. There can be no doubt that in all the various partnerships with his brothers, and also with John Wisden, it was Fred Lillywhite who bore the major responsibility for management. He must have been a man of immense energy to sustain so many diverse activities, all of which were accompanied by a somewhat heavy-handed flair for self-promotion and publicity. His many self-appointed tasks cannot have been helped by his own capability to upset people and become embroiled in dispute and argument. Just one example came in 1865 when the MCC withdrew their patronage of the *Guide to Cricketers* because Lillywhite's published comments on Parr and Wisden 'exceeded the fair limits of criticism'.

Of all those involved in the Anderson lithographs, the fourth person in the publishing credits, John Wisden, is undoubtedly the most famous today by virtue of the almanack that carries his name. In the 1850s, however, he was just one of many leading cricketers of the day, and his fame as a publisher and sports goods supplier lay in the future. In the period from October 1855 to 1858 Wisden was in partnership with Fred Lillywhite at 2, New Coventry Street, Leicester Square, for the sale of cricket equipment and cigars and it was through this liaison that his name appears on many of the lithographs. Even during this period, however, there can be little doubt that it was Fred Lillywhite who provided the driving force behind the continuation of the Anderson series. To him, whatever his faults as an individual, is owed a tremendous debt of gratitude by all who have admired the pictures over the years.

# The Lithographs

At first sight the variety of sizes, colours, publishers, printers and titles of the Anderson lithographs can appear confusing. The Catalogue that follows these notes seeks to clarify the history of the prints and make identification easier by following a chronological approach. Since many of the lithographs show no date of publication, much of the necessary information has been gleaned from contemporary reports and advertisements.

Each lithograph has been given a unique number to enable convenient reference. Identification of a particular print can best be made by reference first to the index of players' names and then to the relevant Catalogue entry.

While there may be publishing variations that have escaped the attention of the compilers of this Catalogue, it is unlikely that Anderson produced lithographs of any cricketers other than those listed. Anderson himself claimed that he had sketched forty-two cricketers but that not all were published. The current list covers thirty-nine different players, including Hunt and Wright who appeared only in the group portrait of the United All England XI.

## 1850

Anderson's first cricketing portrait, 'James Henry Dark – the Proprietor of Lord's', was published on 20 May 1850 and was followed by a further four during the remainder of the summer. These first lithographs had a printed area of approximately 29cm × 22cm and an overall sheet size of 43cm × 30cm, the format which later became known as the 'Large Series'. The lithographs were printed by the prestigious firm of Hullmandel and Walton, and published by Anderson and Robert Dark. At this stage the young Fred Lillywhite was not credited as co-publisher, but his travelling printing tent provided one of the main outlets for the sale of the pictures. The prints were also available from Robert Dark himself and from leading London dealers such as Rudolph Ackermann and Fore & Company.

Each of the first five issues – Dark, Caldecourt, Hillyer, Martingell and Adams – was available plain (i.e. with a buff-coloured tint) at 2s 6d, or hand coloured for 4s od. The early advertisements (example reproduced below) stated that the lithographs would be published fortnightly, but this does not quite tally with the dates shown on the prints.

On MAY 20 will be published the first Number of a series of full-length
Portraits, entitled
**"SKETCHES AT LORD'S;"**
BY JOHN CORBET ANDERSON.
No. 1
**Mr. JAMES HENRY DARK,**
Proprietor of Lord's Ground.
No. 2 will be
**"THE UMPIRE,"**
WILLIAM CALDECOURT.
*These Sketches will be continued every fortnight, and will contain full-length Portraits of the most celebrated Noblemen, Gentlemen, and Professional Players.*
Price: Plain 2s. 6d., Coloured 4s.
Published by JOHN CORBET ANDERSON, 40, Church-road, De Beauvoir-square, Kingsland; and Mr. ROBERT DARK, Tennis Court, Lord's Ground, London.
May be had also of F. LILLYWHITE, at his Printing Tent, at all the Grand Matches with All England.

*Advertisement for the very first in the Anderson series
of famous cricketers.*

It is important to note that these first five Large Series lithographs usually carry the title 'Sketches at Lord's', along with the appropriate number, around the arched border at the top of the print, although there were variants, at least of Martingell and Adams, in which this wording is completely missing. This title was used in contemporary reviews and advertisements and was obviously intended for a whole series of 'full-length portraits of the most celebrated noblemen, gentlemen and professional players'. Strangely, the words 'Sketches at Lord's' were dropped for subsequent Large Series issues and the title is now best known from the twelve Small Series lithographs produced by Anderson in 1852. A catchy title, presumably devised by Anderson or Robert Dark, it could have been prompted by the widely sold book *Sketches of the Players*, produced by the reporter William Denison only four years earlier.

There was also a set of lithographs produced by Mourilyan and Casey entitled 'Sketches at Lord's Ground No. 1, 2,' etc., and these can be confused with Anderson's lithographs if improperly catalogued. They are, in fact, poor quality pirated versions based on some of Anderson's prints and on those of Basébe. Since they are undated we cannot be certain who first thought of the phrase 'Sketches at Lord's', but the derivative and shoddy nature of all other

*In a blatant example of pirating, Mourilyan and Casey
here superimpose Alfred Mynn's face on a mirror image
of Lillywhite's body.*

aspects of the Mourilyan and Casey lithographs suggests that they probably also copied Anderson's title.

Incidentally, although the title sounds very appropriate, it is actually far from accurate. The majority of Anderson's original portraits were executed in the grounds of the Three Tuns public house in The Borough, where most of the professionals stayed when playing in London. It is true that the first four in the series – Dark, Caldecourt, Hillyer and Martingell – show various parts of Lord's Ground in the background but in virtually all the subsequent lithographs Anderson used a variety of tents, churches and windmills to add interest to the scene. Only in the case of the large version of William Lillywhite did he revert to the Lord's theme, and then only because the print commemorated the Great Man's benefit match held at the ground.

Returning to that first appearance of James Dark's portrait on 20 May, *Bell's Life* reviewed the new venture enthusiastically:

Sketches at Lord's – we have seen the first of a series of full-length lithographic portraits, under this title, which has just been published by Mr Robert Dark of Lord's Ground. They are by Mr J. C. Anderson, a pupil of the lamented Haydon, and are intended to comprise the most celebrated noblemen, gentlemen and professional players of the day. Mr James Henry Dark, the well-known proprietor of Lord's, is the

first selected, and if any criterion of the skill of this very talented young artist was
wanted, it is given in this excellent portrait. The likeness to us appears perfect, the
figure characteristically brought out and artistically executed, and the background
displays the arena on which so many noble struggles for victory have been contested
by the elite of the cricketing world; while the whole is so beautifully and truthfully
delineated, as to render this sketch an agreeable refresher to those who have crowded
to this ground 'many times and oft' to witness the exploits performed thereon.
Judging by No. 1, the decided success of 'Sketches at Lord's' is no doubt certain.

This and many subsequent admiring reviews were doubtless written or
inspired by Fred Lillywhite, the *Bell's Life* cricket reporter, who was never
slow to give publicity to any of his own ventures or items available from his
various businesses.

The second portrait in the series – that of William Caldecourt, the most
famous umpire of the day – was duly published a fortnight after the first, on
3 June 1850, although the date given on the lithograph itself is 20 May. The
fortnightly sequence was also maintained for the third issue – William
Hillyer, published on 17 June. This was the first of the series to show an active
cricketer, and *Bell's Life* commented that Anderson 'seems to improve with
his subject', adding that:

. . . the portrait is an excellent likeness, the attitude is easy and the character and style
of the figure so true to the original that the 'Pride of Kent's bowlers' stands forth to
his numerous admirers in life-like portraiture. They are executed in a style that
speaks much for the rising talent of the young artist, and the first rate printing by
Hullmandel and Walton does the greatest credit to their establishment.

The output during this first year was completed by the portraits of Martingell
and Adams, who may not be household names today but were at this time,
like Hillyer, among the very best cricketers of the day. The print of Adams is
probably inferior to the others from an artistic point of view, the pose
appearing somewhat awkward and ungainly, and this probably accounts for
its comparative rarity today.

# 1851

Encouraged by the success of these first five lithographs, Anderson and Dark
embarked on a second series with only a few minor changes. The contemporary advertising still referred to 'Sketches at Lord's', but the prints themselves
no longer carried the title. The Catalogue in this book shows the dates printed
on the lithographs, but again contemporary advertisements tell a slightly
different story. The first three issues were announced for publication on
5 May and were described as 'Sketches at Lord's' No. 6 – Guy, No. 7 – Parr,
and No. 8 – Clarke. Later in the summer came lithographs of Alfred Mynn

and Fuller Pilch, and it was announced that these five famous names would comprise Anderson's total output for the year. In August, however, Harry Sampson's portrait appeared, a late addition that might have been prompted by Fred Lillywhite, whose name had by now appeared in the publishing credits in place of Robert Dark.

*A lithograph of Daniel Day, similar in style to Anderson's work but, in fact, by Felix.*

A further mystery concerning this period is the slight possibility that there may have been an Anderson lithograph of Daniel Day, the Hampshire and Surrey cricketer. Day's name was included in Fred Lillywhite's advertisements under the heading 'Cricketers' Likenesses' in the same list as the Anderson portraits (although Anderson is not mentioned by name). In separate advertisements placed by Anderson himself, however, Day is never mentioned. Rockley Wilson, in an article written for *The Cricketer* in 1943, assumed that Lillywhite's lists implied an Anderson lithograph of Day, although he admits it was one of the few he did not possess in his own fine collection. Indeed, no copy has since come to light and it is most likely that Lillywhite's list was referring to a lithograph of Day after a painting by Felix, which appeared in this same year of 1851. According to Ashley-Cooper this print was limited to only twenty-five copies, a fact which would explain its disappearance from later Lillywhite lists. It superficially resembles the Anderson lithographs in style and appearance although larger in size, but it was definitely not produced by or after him.

# 1852

This year saw a new departure for Anderson. Instead of continuing with the previous format he released three larger sheets (overall size 48cm × 37cm), each containing four separate, smaller portraits (approximately 18cm × 12cm). These, and later similar issues, were known as the 'Small Series'. For the twelve initial studies the title 'Sketches at Lord's' was restored, and the publishers were Anderson and Fred Lillywhite. A new printer, almost certainly Richard Black, was used. The subjects were repetitions of ten of the eleven previously published Large Series (Adams was omitted, perhaps because it was clearly the least attractive) with the addition of Wisden and Box – both highly celebrated cricketers who had not appeared before. The new small versions of Dark, Caldecourt, Hillyer and Martingell retained the titles 'Sketches at Lord's' Numbers 1, 2, 3 and 4 respectively, as they had in the Large Series of 1850, and the remainder were allocated numbers from 5 to 12. The composition of these small portraits is very similar to the large versions, although they were obviously made from different lithographic stones and the occasional minor difference is detectable. The captions are slightly different and Sampson's name is misspelt by the omission of the 'p'. The most noticeable change occurred with the removal of the stumps from the small version of Joseph Guy.

The Small Series prints are perhaps the most frequently encountered Andersons today, and they must have sold in large numbers. At 5s 0d for a sheet of four (6s 6d coloured) they were considerably cheaper to purchase than the large style. They are nearly always found singly now, but there is no doubt they were originally produced from a single stone as sheets of four. Only Wisden and Box were advertised as being available separately (at 1s 6d each), perhaps because they were the two new subjects. This must have resulted in others from those sheets also being sold individually, but even so they would have been cut from the original large sheet and do not constitute separate lithographs.

The definitive series of 'Sketches at Lord's' was issued surprisingly early – 1 March – and nothing more was seen until July when further variety was introduced into the format. This time four players were represented in a single picture under the title 'Sketches of the Surrey Cricketers'. Shortly afterwards another sheet with four of the Small Series portraits was issued with no title other than the players' names – Grundy, Dean, Chatterton and Nixon.

The output this year was completed by just one portrait of the original larger size, of Charles Brown of Nottingham. This lithograph is very scarce and bears no publisher's name. It was apparently financed by Brown himself, probably for sale in Nottingham where he was secretary to the county club, and it never appeared in any of Fred Lillywhite's lists. *Bell's Life* considered that the portrait 'not only conveys an admirable likeness, but embodies the peculiarity of style of that eccentric player'.

# 1853

The fourth season of Anderson's cricketing works was again a busy one, starting in early April with the publication of another set of four Small Series portraits on a single sheet. This time the subject was dear to Fred Lillywhite's heart – 'Lillywhite and Sons' – and for the first time Anderson was not credited as co-publisher. Fred had been announcing the impending arrival of this particular lithograph for some time and he continued to give it maximum publicity whenever possible. Nevertheless, it is now quite rare and cannot have proved very popular at the time. Like the previous Small Series sheets it sold for 5s 0d, with a hand-coloured version at 6s 6d. No printer is credited, but Richard Black is again most likely.

This summer also saw Anderson return to the Large Series, with individual portraits of Wisden, Caffyn and Lockyer being added to the list, although the image size of the last is somewhat smaller than the others in the series. While Wisden and Lockyer were praised as usual in *Bell's Life* as 'most striking likenesses', Caffyn drew the first faint criticism – 'his face perhaps being rather too full, but all who know the man will recognize it at once'. The portrait of Wisden is almost identical to the previous small version although the shirt front is of a plainer design.

In addition to these new portraits, the original lithograph of Joseph Guy was this year reprinted by Richard Black in a virtually identical composition to the earlier version by Hullmandel and Walton. A different stone was used, however, and since the printing process is so important to the finished lithograph these must be considered as two different works in the Anderson Catalogue. The Caffyn and Lockyer lithographs also underwent minor changes at later dates, but since in each case the only difference was a change in the name of the publisher, the actual lithographs being printed from the original stone, a separate catalogue entry has not been made. In the case of Caffyn this minor variant was issued during the period of the Lillywhite/

Wisden partnership at 2 New Coventry Street (1855–58). That of Lockyer appeared slightly later, when Wisden was operating the business alone from the same address. In both cases the earlier versions, which are quite rare, are clearer and more distinct than the later variants, perhaps indicating some deterioration in the stone or lack of care by the printer.

The final portrait this year was of Thomas Beagley, formerly a leading Hampshire cricketer, who in 1821 had scored the first ever century in Gentlemen *v* Players matches. By 1853 Beagley was aged sixty-three and had fallen on hard times. Because of his unhappy condition, a benefit match was arranged at The Oval between Twenty-two of I Zingari and the All England Eleven, but rain ruined the game and poor Beagley suffered a net loss on the event. This was recovered, however, through a hastily arranged rematch later in the season. As part of the fund-raising efforts, Anderson produced this lithographic portrait to be available by subscription to the benefit. Since the print was never included in later lists by Lillywhite, there were presumably only enough copies produced to supply the subscribers, of whom there were approximately one hundred. This would explain the great rarity of the print today compared with many of the others in the series.

Another, and far more celebrated, benefit match held in 1853 was for William Lillywhite, Fred's illustrious father. On 25 and 26 July at Lord's a very strong and representative England team beat Sussex (with George Parr), and thanks to Fred's talent for promotion, the event was a great success. It was announced at the time that all subscribers to the benefit would receive a daguerreotype portrait of Lillywhite 'as he appeared on the day', but this never materialized. Instead, after a considerable delay Anderson produced a lithograph of the 'Great Man' which was finally sent out to subscribers in April 1854. As with Beagley there were approximately a hundred names on the list, but for Lillywhite many of these donated large amounts of money or involved multiple donations from clubs. Nevertheless, there were probably only about a hundred of these original presentation lithographs produced. Here the similarity with Beagley ends, for in later years the print of Old Lillywhite was repeatedly advertised by his son Fred, and copies have survived in reasonable numbers to the present day. Most of these, however, while carrying the legend 'This Plate is Respectfully Dedicated to the Subscribers', appear to have been published by Lillywhite and Wisden at 2 New Coventry Street, thereby indicating a date between October 1855 and 1858. The versions most often found are therefore probably part of the original print run subsequently labelled with the Lillywhite/Wisden name and address. Indeed, no copy without their name has come to light during the research for this book. The depiction of Old Lillywhite in this lithograph is quite different to the pose used in the earlier small version published on the 'Lillywhite and Sons' sheet.

# 1855

Apart from the Lillywhite benefit print, 1854 appears to have been a blank year for Anderson's cricketing output. Doubtless he was concentrating most of his efforts on producing the lithographs for his first book – *Monuments and Antiquities of Croydon Church* – which was to be published privately by subscription during 1855. Perhaps it was the need to fund this venture that prompted Anderson, at the beginning of 1855, to sell all his remaining stock of the earlier lithographs to Fred Lillywhite for £45. Up to this date Anderson's name had almost always appeared as the main publisher of the prints as well as the original artist and lithographer. Subsequently he must

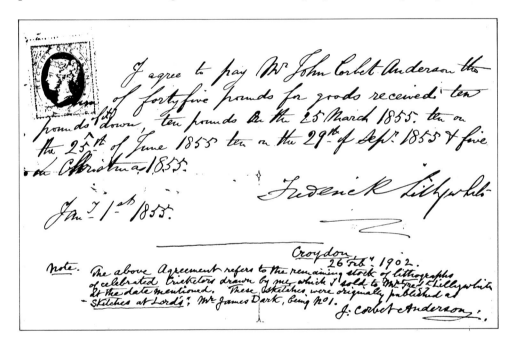

*The original contract between Anderson and Fred Lillywhite.*

have come to a different financial arrangement with Fred Lillywhite as, with the exception of the Bickley lithograph which appeared later in 1855, Anderson was no longer credited as co-publisher.

This sale of Anderson's stock of prints gives some clues regarding the extent of the original print runs. Assuming that a price of £45 assured Lillywhite a healthy profit on their resale, it could correspond to as many as a thousand lithographs, or, on average, about fifty of each. If this was the remaindered stock from the previous five years, then an original printing of two to three hundred for each portrait does not seem unreasonable. It must have been at least this number if we believe that a run of one hundred for the

Beagley print has resulted in its comparative rarity today. Anything appreciably greater than three or four hundred would surely have resulted in far more copies surviving for the modern collector.

Probably it was this acquisition of the complete stock that prompted Fred Lillywhite to reduce the price of the Large Series portraits to 2s 0d plain and 3s 0d coloured (previously 2s 6d and 4s 0d) and the Small Series sheets from 5s 0d to 4s 0d. In a further attempt to boost sales he also advertised that the Large Series 'may also be had in fours, mounted and varnished for the parlour (public or private) – price 10s 6d'. These were, in fact, four of the lithographs mounted side by side in a common frame some four feet wide. The following groupings were available:

> Dark, Mynn, Wisden, Adams
> Caldecourt, Sampson, Caffyn, W. Lillywhite
> Parr, Clarke, Bickley, Guy
> Lockyer, Martingell, Pilch, Hillyer

It is not known whether any of these groups of four has survived in its original frame, but if so it would be a highly prized item.

After the blank year of 1854 it was appropriate that Anderson should produce something out of the ordinary for the following year. On 1 April 1855 the following notice appeared in *Bell's Life*:

The United All England Eleven – Portraits of these celebrated PLAYERS (forming a group of 14) will be ready on 1st May. To subscribers: Plain 10s 6d. Coloured 15s 0d.

This, perhaps the most esteemed of all Anderson's cricketing works, was clearly a massive undertaking – the culmination of his efforts over the previous five years. The review in *Bell's Life* read:

The UNITED ELEVEN – A very spirited lithographic representation of this celebrated team has lately been published by the Lillywhites, which, we doubt not, will find a ready sale among their numerous patrons and admirers. The difficulty of giving to a print of this kind anything like an agreeable effect has been very fairly surmounted, and the likenesses, which is the important point, are good, especially those of Hunt and Wisden. It is from the pencil of John Corbet Anderson, a well-known artist.

This lithograph was the first of Anderson's to be printed by the firm of Stannard and Dixon, and he was to remain with them for all his subsequent cricket works. The date of the picture has always been the subject of some conjecture, since it is not given on the print and the players do not represent the team for a particular match but are an artificial compilation of the best to represent the United Eleven around this time. But the publication date can now be firmly established as 1 May 1855, and the picture was certainly up to date since William Caffyn did not begin playing for the United Eleven until the summer of 1855. The original painting has the date 1852 written in ink after Anderson's signature but this is clearly in a later hand and is almost certainly an error.

## 1856–60

During the three years from 1856 to 1858 the partnership of Lillywhite and Wisden was flourishing, and the publication of Anderson's lithographs continued under their joint name. Each year saw two or three new prints in the Large Series, and there was a new printing by Stannard and Dixon of the famous Alfred Mynn portrait from 1851. The lithographs of John Lillywhite and Dean showed, however, totally different poses to the Small Series versions of several years earlier.

After the break-up of the Lillywhite/Wisden partnership there was a brief hiatus, but the incorrigible Fred was soon back in business and publishing under his own name again. Hearne, Griffith and Mortlock were added to the list and a new version of George Parr was produced, but the comparative rarity of these later issues indicates that sales were falling off. Perhaps the rarest of all is the lithograph of Henry Royston which was published by the player himself, possibly for his benefit in 1861. There was once a copy in the MCC collection (see *Lord's and the MCC* by Lord Harris and F. S. Ashley-Cooper), but this has now disappeared.

The era of the lithograph was rapidly coming to an end and the public demanded the new-fangled 'photographs' which were appearing with increasing regularity. In 1858 *Bell's Life* had concluded its review of Anderson's lithograph of Stephenson with the question, 'Why should not cricketers "submit their mugs to the camera" as well as rowing and other sporting men?' The following year Fred Lillywhite himself took up this challenge and published the famous photograph by Hennah of the 1859 team which toured the USA and Canada. This was soon to be followed by a flood of cricket photographs showing team groups and individual players.

By 1860 Anderson was approaching the end of his cricketing period and had essentially run out of commercially attractive subjects for the standard portrait. In an attempt to raise the flagging sales, and doubtless at the instigation of Fred Lillywhite, he tried two interesting changes to the previous format. The first depicts a pleasant scene in which the late William Lillywhite is bowling to youngsters outside the family cottage – 'Teaching the young idea how to shoot' as Fred Lillywhite described it in an advertisement. This was available, as before, in both tinted (2s 6d) and hand-coloured (3s od)

*One of the earliest cricket photographs, by Hennah, depicts
nine of Anderson's cricketers in the 1859 touring team.
Left to right: Carpenter, Caffyn, Lockyer, Wisden, Stephenson,
Parr, Grundy, Caesar, Hayward, Jackson.
Seated: Diver and John Lillywhite.*

*'Lillywhite at Home.'*

form. While the print must have provided a happy reminiscence for the Lillywhite family, it was hardly likely to command a huge sale – a pity, since a varied selection of cricket scenes from Anderson could have been very attractive.

The other principal project in 1860 was something of a disappointment – a series of eight 'Cricketing Postures'. These are clearly derived from the much earlier series by G. F. Watts and the illustrations to Nicholas Wanostrocht's book *Felix on the Bat*. They were available plain or coloured, but the plain versions appear to have lacked the usual tint. This certainly detracts from their appearance, and they have a 'flat' quality compared with the classic images of Watts. It is hard to see why Anderson should have chosen such a derivative theme, but perhaps Fred Lillywhite had detected a market for these updated versions. If so he must have miscalculated, as their comparative scarcity today indicates that sales must have been poor. Certainly they seem to have convinced both artist and publisher that the heyday of the cricket lithograph was over. This was perhaps a sad way for Anderson to end a decade of artistic achievement the rest of which has certainly stood the test of time.

Apart from the long list of portraits produced during this eleven-year period, Anderson was also responsible for a handful of other cricket subjects that are today exceedingly rare. One of the earliest was a panoramic view of Lord's Ground published by Robert Dark and printed by Hullmandel and Walton. An accurate piece of draughtsmanship rather than artistically inspired, the copy in the MCC collection has the year 1851 written in by hand.

Music and song covers of this period occasionally featured cricketing lithographs, and at least one such was the work of Anderson. The 'Merry Cricketers Polka' was published in 1853 and depicted the secretary of the St John's Cricket Club in a pose typical of so many of Anderson's more famous portraits.

Two other lithographs, titled 'The Romford Cricket Club' and 'The City of London Cricket Club', were produced by Anderson but are virtually unobtainable today, indeed no copy of the latter has been found during the research for this book. Both were in the pre-war collection of Lt Col Sloane-Stanley which later passed to Walter Hutchinson (see page 43 *et seq.*), but it was not identified in the 1952 sale catalogue of that collection and has not since come to light. The Romford and City clubs played against each other in regular fixtures around the years 1848 to 1852, and in all probability these two lithographs were executed for private circulation to the members of the two clubs.

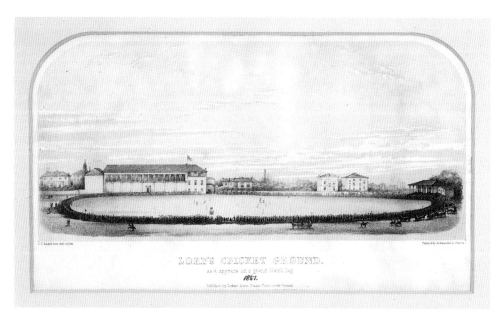

This Anderson lithograph of Lord's Ground is an important
view of the ground in 1851 and can be compared with a slightly later
watercolour by Nathaniel Green, now in the Melbourne Club's collection.

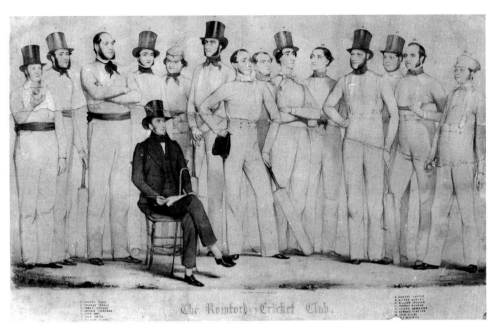

*The Romford Cricket Club –*
*one of the rarest of Anderson's lithographs,*
*and probably his first cricketing work.*

*A pirated but faithful reproduction of Anderson's work.*

The Romford print is undated but from the identity of the players the year is almost certainly 1849 which could make it Anderson's first cricketing work. Interestingly, there are references at this time to an Anderson playing in the City team but whether this was a relation, or even young Corbet himself, is impossible to determine. Certainly, in later life he never claimed any prowess at the game. The connection with the City club is not surprising since at this time Anderson was living within a mile of the club's ground in Islington. Furthermore, Fred Lillywhite's premises were just down the road in Prince's Terrace.

One final curiosity, a copy of which is in the Nottinghamshire CCC collection at Trent Bridge, was a pirated version of Anderson's work titled 'Sketches of the Nottingham Cricketers'. This interesting composite was very much a local Nottingham production; Anderson is not credited on the lithograph and presumably had no part in its production. The publisher, George Cummings, employed Henry Yates as lithographer and the firm of Davis as printers – all three operated in Nottingham during the mid-1850s when the print was probably produced.

### Notes for Collectors

Obviously any of the Anderson lithographs are highly desirable collectors' items if found in good condition, and they will usually command a correspondingly high price. Nevertheless, some of the prints are encountered more often than others while some are virtually unobtainable. It is doubtful whether any collector, either club or individual, has ever assembled the complete works as catalogued here. Rockley Wilson was only missing a few, and doubtless others, notably MCC, could have achieved a complete set given the information now presented for the first time.

Probably the most frequently found are the twelve Small Series portraits titled 'Sketches at Lord's', although these are rarely in their original state of four to a sheet. Of the Large Series, Guy (1853 version) and Hillyer seem the most common, with Dean and Diver also quite often found. All the others can be considered rare, especially the non-Lillywhite publications such as Brown, Royston and Beagley. The larger lithographs – 'Sketches of the Surrey Cricketers' and 'The United All England Eleven' – have rarely survived in good condition and would probably fetch the highest prices of all Anderson's works.

## ORIGINAL SKETCHES

As we have seen, Anderson claimed to have painted the portraits of forty-two different cricketers, although not all were lithographed. Since a number of players were apparently sketched more than once, he probably produced at least fifty originals, twenty-four of which can be found either at Lord's or in private collections. Of the rest there is apparently no trace but surely some must have survived, either proudly on a collector's wall or anonymously in a dusty attic. Probably the greatest prize, the original painting of the United All England Eleven, was passed after Anderson's death to one of the artist's six children, who lived in Canada. It has since found its way into the MCC Collection at Lord's but it is intriguing to speculate whether other paintings are still giving pleasure to a subsequent generation of Andersons in that country. In reality, however, most of the untraced original sketches have probably been permanently lost or destroyed, just as, so Anderson claimed, the original lithographic stones were eventually used to pave streets and passageways in London.

The known sketches are of two main types – either true watercolour paintings on beige paper (approximately 37cm × 27cm) or much larger line and wash drawings on white paper (66cm × 38cm). Only six of the latter type appear to have survived, all dated 1852, presumably studies for the Small Series 'Sketches at Lord's' which appeared that year. All twenty-four are signed and titled, and all but two are dated. With the exception of Bickley, they seem to have been painted in the same year as the lithograph was published. It is not clear why duplicate sketches were needed, but at least Wisden and Pilch were done in each of the two different styles. The complete list of known line and wash drawings is: Sampson, Dark, Pilch, Martingell, Wisden and Hillyer. The other smaller sketches discovered to date are: Clarke, Guy, Parr, Pilch, Box, Sketches of the Surrey Cricketers, Wisden, Lillywhite (F. W.), Lockyer, Caffyn, Bickley, The United Eleven of All England, Hankey, Willsher, Mynn, Stephenson, Miller and Caesar.

We have mentioned elsewhere that the sketches were often produced at the Three Tuns public house where Alfred Mynn had shocked the youthful Anderson with his prodigious appetite during a two-and-a-half-hour sitting. Whether Anderson subsequently kept the originals, sold them or gave them to the subject we will never know. The earliest provenance that can be traced concerns eighteen of the sketches which for many years were in the magnificent Sloane-Stanley collection. This name is hardly known today, but during the first half of the twentieth century Lt Col. Ronald Francis Asshton Sloane-Stanley amassed a stunning array of cricket paintings, drawings and prints. Educated at Eton and Sandhurst, Sloane-Stanley was severely wounded in the Boer War and this prematurely ended his military career. Thereafter he lived for many years in retirement in Cowes, Isle of Wight, where he could indulge his two great passions – yachting and collecting cricket pictures. It was there that he died in 1948, aged eighty. It is not known where he acquired the Anderson sketches, but he was a regular buyer from the leading dealers and

*A line and wash drawing of James Henry Dark.*
*This can be compared with the smaller watercolour technique*
*seen in the sketch of Julius Caesar on page 13.*

sale rooms. His collecting successes, in an era when Sir Jeremiah Colman was acquiring similar material with single-minded determination, were impressive. He bought many of the original sketches for the *Vanity Fair* cartoons when the magazine sold them at auction in 1912, and also possessed numerous other important paintings and drawings and virtually every worthwhile lithograph and engraving on the game.

When Sloane-Stanley died in 1948, the MCC was offered the chance to buy the collection. Col. R. S. Rait Kerr, the club secretary, and H. S. Altham went down to Hampshire for an initial inspection, quickly followed by Diana Rait Kerr, the colonel's daughter and curator of the MCC collection. The MCC had seldom purchased expensive items, its magnificent collection having been built mainly from donations. The library had been based on two major bequests – those of A. L. Ford and F. S. Ashley-Cooper (via Sir Julian Cahn) – and the club had just received the first instalment of the late Sir Jeremiah Colman's pictures. In light of this, only a relatively small number of pictures were finally chosen and taken back to Lord's, where they were valued by Sotheby's at £696. The negotiations between the MCC and the Sloane-Stanley estate became rather protracted, but the deal appeared to have gone through when suddenly the executors accepted a counter offer of £3500 for the entire collection. The buyer, who lost no time in removing the items which had by then been stored at Lord's for some months, was Walter Hutchinson, publisher and sportsman, an intriguing figure who thereby became the new possessor of eighteen Anderson sketches and virtually all of the lithographs.

Born in 1887, Hutchinson had originally trained as a barrister before taking control of the family publishing house. There he turned Hutchinsons into a highly successful business by ignoring old-fashioned publishing practices and regarding books as a simple commodity. In many ways he was a forerunner of today's publishers – he acquired other firms voraciously and concentrated on mass appeal rather than pure literary merit. Outside the business world he had two great passions – the breeding and racing of horses and the collecting of sporting pictures. Originally he concentrated on equine pictures, but later extended his interest to include all sports and pastimes. With the Sloane-Stanley collection he was able, at a stroke, to acquire probably the finest collection of cricket pictures outside Lord's. Even such long-standing collectors as Joe Goldman and Rockley Wilson could hardly match this unique treasure trove.

During the Second World War Hutchinson had evolved the idea of making his magnificent collection permanently available for exhibition to the public. In 1946 he bought Derby House, an impressive Adam building in Stratford Place, London. He renamed it Hutchinson House and eventually, in February 1949, unveiled his 'National Gallery of British Sports and Pastimes'. Initially about six hundred pictures were displayed out of a total collection of some three thousand. Most, including a number by Stubbs and Herring, reflected Hutchinson's love for horses, but he was rapidly planning the inclusion of the recently acquired Sloane-Stanley material. In the summer of 1950 a special Cricket Exhibition was opened, including seventeen of the Anderson original sketches and ten of the lithographs – the first and only time that such a selection of the artist's work has been seen publicly. Sadly, Hutchinson did not live to see the exhibition open, dying at the early age of sixty-two on 30 April that year. The driving force behind the Gallery was gone, and despite mounting a small exhibition of sporting trophies in 1951, the decision was soon taken to sell the collection in a series of three sales at Christie's.

It was at the last, and smallest, of these sales that the Anderson material changed hands for the second time in four years, and for once there were real bargains to be had. The collection, dominated by a Constable plus the Stubbs and Herrings, fetched over £130,000, but the Anderson sketches went for the proverbial song. The first lot – two large line and wash drawings of Hillyer and Wisden – were bought by Diana Rait Kerr on behalf of the MCC for twenty-six guineas, and can be seen today in the members' writing room at Lord's. The other sixteen sketches were knocked down in five lots for a staggeringly low total of only fifty-four guineas. These same lots even included the rare lithographs of the Surrey Cricketers and the Four Lillywhites, plus two large watercolours by Basébe as a bonus!

The lucky recipient of this windfall was a noted private collector, bidding through an agent. He was not able to attend the sale but simply instructed the London dealers, Maggs Bros, to spend up to an agreed limit and obtain whatever they could of the finer cricket items, which he marked in the catalogue. The next day the collector was far from optimistic when he telephoned Maggs to learn whether he had been successful with any of the preferred lots. His reaction can be imagined when he was greeted with the news that he had bought all of them! In fact, a total of 158 guineas had enabled him to acquire sixteen Anderson sketches, fourteen *Vanity Fair* originals, and nineteen other paintings and drawings including two by G. F. Watts. A series of circumstances had led to the sort of coup that all collectors dream of but which so seldom seems to happen. The leading cricket picture collectors – Sloane-Stanley, Hutchinson, Colman – were no longer alive, and the dealers present were clearly unsure of the market. The other active collectors, however, including Joe Goldman, Rockley Wilson, John Arlott, Desmond Eagar, Neville Weston, E. G. Wolfe and others, must surely have cast envious eyes on the rich haul. The Anderson sketches were kept in their new home for many years, but have now found treasured places in a number of other private collections.

One misleading reference concerns a painting of the umpire and former Nottinghamshire player Thomas Barker. This oil on canvas work was reproduced in a 1956 issue of *Country Life*, where it was tentatively attributed to Anderson. This statement was repeated in *The Art of Cricket* by Simon and Smart, but the style of the picture is so unlike any of Anderson's known works that the attribution can probably be discounted.

Perhaps there are other Anderson sketches or paintings in existence, and it is to be hoped that this book might stimulate their discovery. As with all the unique items beloved by cricket collectors, the sixteen known Andersons still in private hands will continue to pass from one generation to the next. One thing is certain, however – they will never again change hands for an average of three pounds each!

# Catalogue of Lithographs

| | TITLE | PRINTER | PUBLISHER | DATE | SIZE (cm) |
|---|---|---|---|---|---|
| 1 | M<sup>R</sup> JAMES HENRY DARK<br>Proprietor of Lord's Cricket Ground<br>(Sketches at Lord's No. 1) | HW | JCA/RD | 20/5/50 | 29 × 22 |
| 2 | THE UMPIRE<br>(W. H. Caldecourt)<br>(Sketches at Lord's No. 2) | HW | JCA/RD | 20/5/50 | 29 × 22 |
| 3 | HILLYER<br>(Sketches at Lord's No. 3) | HW | JCA/RD | 17/6/50 | 29 × 22 |
| 4 | MARTINGELL<br>Born 20<sup>th</sup> August, 1818, at Nutfield in Surrey<br>(Sketches at Lord's No. 4) | HW | JCA/RD | 8/7/50 | 29 × 22 |
| 5 | ADAMS<br>(Sketches at Lord's No. 5) | HW | JCA/RD | 22/7/50 | 31 × 22 |
| 6 | GEORGE PARR | HW | JCA/RD | 15/4/51 | 31 × 23 |
| 7 | JOSEPH GUY<br>of Nottingham | HW | JCA/RD | 20/5/51 | 30 × 22 |
| 8 | W. CLARKE<br>Slow Bowler<br>Sect<sup>y</sup> to the All England Team | HW | JCA/RD | 20/5/51 | 32 × 23 |
| 9 | A. MYNN ESQ<sup>RE</sup> | HW | – | (June 1851) | – |
| 10 | FULLER PILCH | HW | JCA/FL | 1/7/51 | 30 × 22 |
| 11 | SAMPSON<br>of Sheffield | HW | JCA/FL | 1/8/51 | 31 × 22 |
| 12a | M<sup>R</sup> JAMES HENRY DARK<br>Proprietor of Lord's Cricket Ground<br>(Sketches at Lord's No. 1) | – | JCA/FL | 1/3/52 | 18 × 13 |
| 12b | THE UMPIRE<br>William Caldecourt, born at Blisworth in 1802<br>(Sketches at Lord's No. 2) | – | JCA/FL | 1/3/52 | 18 × 13 |
| 12c | HILLYER<br>Born at Leybourne, Kent<br>(Sketches at Lord's No. 3) | – | JCA/FL | 1/3/52 | 18 × 13 |

| | TITLE | PRINTER | PUBLISHER | DATE | SIZE (cm) |
|---|---|---|---|---|---|
| 12d | MARTINGELL<br>Born at Nutfield, Surrey, 1818<br>(Sketches at Lord's No. 4) | – | JCA/FL | 1/3/52 | 18 × 13 |
| 13a | ALFRED MYNN ESQ<sup>RE</sup><br>Born Near Cranbrook, Kent<br>(Sketches at Lord's No. 5) | – | JCA/FL | 1/3/52 | 19 × 12 |
| 13b | WISDEN<br>Born at Brighton<br>(Sketches at Lord's No. 6) | – | JCA/FL | 1/3/52 | 18 × 12 |
| 13c | FULLER PILCH<br>of Canterbury. Born 1803. Height 6ft ½in<br>(Sketches at Lord's No. 7) | – | JCA/FL | 1/3/52 | 17 × 12 |
| 13d | SAMSON<br>of Sheffield<br>Height 5ft 4in<br>(Sketches at Lord's No. 8) | – | JCA/FL | 1/3/52 | 18 × 12 |
| 14a | BOX<br>Born at Ardingley, Sussex, 1809<br>Height 5ft 7in<br>(Sketches at Lord's No. 9) | – | JCA/FL | 1/3/52 | 17 × 12 |
| 14b | GEORGE PARR<br>Born at Radcliff, near Nottingham, 1826<br>Height 5ft 9in<br>(Sketches at Lord's No. 10) | – | JCA/FL | 1/3/52 | 17 × 12 |
| 14c | JOSEPH GUY<br>Born at Nottingham in 1814<br>Height 5ft 9in<br>(Sketches at Lord's No. 11) | – | JCA/FL | 1/3/52 | 17 × 12 |
| 14d | CLARKE<br>Slow bowler of Nottingham<br>Secretary to the All England Eleven<br>(Sketches at Lord's No. 12) | – | JCA/FL | 1/3/52 | 17 × 12 |
| 15 | SKETCHES OF THE SURREY<br>CRICKETERS | RB | JCA/FL | 16/7/52 | 30 × 34 |
| 16a | GRUNDY | RB | JCA/FL | 23/7/52 | 19 × 12 |
| 16b | DEAN | RB | JCA/FL | 23/7/52 | 17 × 12 |

| | TITLE | PRINTER | PUBLISHER | DATE | SIZE (cm) |
|---|---|---|---|---|---|
| 16c | CHATTERTON | RB | JCA/FL | 23/7/52 | 19 × 11 |
| 16d | NIXON | RB | JCA/FL | 23/7/52 | 17 × 11 |
| 17 | CHARLES BROWN<br>of Nottingham | RB | – | (July 1852) | 27 × 21 |
| 18a | WILLIAM LILLYWHITE<br>Born 1792, at Goodwood – Sufsex | – | FL | (April 1853) | 18 × 12 |
| 18b | FREDERICK LILLYWHITE<br>Born 1829, at Hove near Brighton, Sufsex | – | FL | (April 1853) | 18 × 12 |
| 18c | JAMES LILLYWHITE<br>Born 1825 at Hove near Brighton, Sufsex | – | FL | (April 1853) | 18 × 12 |
| 18d | JOHN LILLYWHITE<br>Born 1826 at Hove near Brighton, Sufsex | – | FL | (April 1853) | 18 × 12 |
| 19 | WISDEN<br>Born at Brighton | RB | JCA/FL | 1/4/53 | 28 × 20 |
| 20 | JOSEPH GUY<br>of Nottingham | RB | JCA/FL | 2/4/53 | 29 × 21 |
| 21 | LOCKYER | RB | JCA/FL | 1/5/53 | 26 × 19 |
| 22 | CAFFYN<br>Born at Reigate, Surrey, Feb$^y$ 2$^{nd}$ 1828 | RB | JCA/FL | 25/7/53 | 30 × 20 |
| 23 | THOMAS BEAGLEY<br>The once celebrated Hampshire Cricketer . . . etc. | RB | – | (July 1853) | 30 × 22 |
| 24 | WILLIAM LILLYWHITE<br>Born June 13$^{th}$ 1792<br>as he appeared at Lord's Ground . . . etc. | RB | FL/JW | (April 1854) | 29 × 19 |
| 25 | THE UNITED ALL ENGLAND ELEVEN | SD | FL | (May 1855) | 44 × 60 |
| 26 | BICKLEY<br>Bowler | SD | JCA/FL | (1855) | 30 × 19 |
| 27 | REGINALD HANKEY ESQ$^{RE}$ | SD | FL/JW | (May 1856) | 31 × 22 |
| 28 | JOHN LILLYWHITE<br>Born 1826, at Hove near Brighton, Sufsex | SD | FL/JW | (May 1856) | 28 × 21 |

| | TITLE | PRINTER | PUBLISHER | DATE | SIZE (cm) |
|---|---|---|---|---|---|
| 29 | F. P. MILLER ESQ<sup>RE</sup> | SD | FL/JW | (May 1856) | 29 × 21 |
| 30 | EDGAR WILLSHER<br>Born at Rolvenden, Kent, Nov<sup>r</sup> 22<sup>nd</sup> 1828 | SD | FL/JW | 2/4/57 | 33 × 23 |
| 31 | JAMES DEAN<br>Born at Duncton, Sussex, 1816 | SD | FL/JW | 14/4/57 | 30 × 21 |
| 32 | ALFRED MYNN ESQ<sup>RE</sup> | SD | FL/JW | 10/8/57 | 32 × 22 |
| 33 | HEATHFIELD HARMAN STEPHENSON<br>Born May 3<sup>rd</sup> 1833, at Esher, Surrey | SD | FL/JW | 12/3/58 | 30 × 21 |
| 34 | JULIUS CÆSAR<br>Born at Godalming, Surrey, March 25<sup>th</sup> 1830 | SD | FL/JW | 24/6/58 | 29 × 20 |
| 35 | ALFRED DIVER<br>Born at Cambridge, July 6<sup>th</sup> 1824 | SD | FL/JW | 18/7/58 | 29 × 19 |
| 36 | T. HEARNE<br>Born at Chalfont St Peter's, Bucks, Sep<sup>t</sup> 4<sup>th</sup> 1826 | SD | FL | 1859 | 30 × 21 |
| 37 | GEORGE GRIFFITH<br>Born at Ripley, Surrey, December 20<sup>th</sup> 1833 | SD | FL | (1860) | 31 × 22 |
| 38 | W. MORTLOCK<br>Born at Kennington, July 18<sup>th</sup> 1832 | SD | FL | (1860) | 31 × 20 |
| 39 | GEORGE PARR | SD | FL | (1859 or 1860) | 31 × 21 |
| 40 | H. ROYSTON<br>of Harrow | SD | – | – | 30 × 19 |
| 41 | STANDING IN ATTITUDE<br>No. 1 | SD | FL | 1/5/60 | 24 × 19 |
| 42 | THE DRAW<br>No. 2 | SD | FL | 1/5/60 | 22 × 19 |
| 43 | THE CUT<br>No. 3 | – | FL | 1/5/60 | 23 × 19 |
| 44 | LEG HIT<br>No. 4 | SD | FL | 1/5/60 | 20 × 19 |
| 45 | FORWARD PLAY<br>No. 5 | SD | FL | 1/5/60 | 20 × 19 |

| | TITLE | PRINTER | PUBLISHER | DATE | SIZE (cm) |
|---|---|---|---|---|---|
| 46 | BACK PLAY<br>No. 6 | SD | FL | 1/5/60 | 23 × 19 |
| 47 | THE BOWLER<br>No. 7 | SD | FL | 1/5/60 | 20 × 19 |
| 48 | THE WICKET KEEPER<br>No. 8 | SD | FL | 1/5/60 | 19 × 19 |
| 49 | LORD'S CRICKET GROUND, AS IT<br>APPEARS ON A GRAND MATCH DAY | HW | RD | (1851) | 14 × 32 |
| 50 | THE MERRY CRICKETERS POLKA<br>Composed and Dedicated to the Members of the<br>St John's Cricket Club by R. Desanges | RB | Rudall, Rose,<br>Carte | (1853) | ? |
| 51 | LILLYWHITE AT HOME<br>A Reminiscence of the Past – A sketch of the<br>Cottage in which the family were born | SD | FL | (May<br>1860) | 15 × 19 |
| 52 | THE CITY OF LONDON CRICKET CLUB | ? | ? | ? | ? |
| 53 | THE ROMFORD CRICKET CLUB | – | – | – | 40 × 65 |

KEY

| | | | |
|---|---|---|---|
| HW | – Hullmandel & Walton | RD | – Robert Dark |
| RB | – Richard Black | FL | – Frederick Lillywhite |
| SD | – Stannard & Dixon | JW | – John Wisden |
| JCA | – John Corbet Anderson | | |

Date in parentheses indicates that this is not given on
the print but gleaned from other sources.
Size excludes margins and text.

NOTES:

4, 5 Also printed without the title 'Sketches at Lord's'
12a, 12b, 12c, 12d Originally on a single sheet, size 48 × 37cm
13a, 13b, 13c, 13d Originally on a single sheet, size 48 × 37cm
14a, 14b, 14c, 14d Originally on a single sheet, size 48 × 37cm
16a, 16b, 16c, 16d Originally on a single sheet, size 47 × 35cm
18a, 18b, 18c, 18d Originally on a single sheet, size 47 × 36cm
21 Later version published by JW – no date – 23 × 18cm
22 Later version published by FL/JW – no date – 29 × 20cm
43 Printer's name not shown but certainly Stannard & Dixon
52 Not seen by Authors

---

# The Players

Many of the players appear in more than one lithograph. This index shows the Catalogue number with the page on which it is reproduced, where appropriate, in parentheses.

# THOMAS MILES ADAMS

Born 2 May 1813, died 20 January 1894

Kent, All England, and United All England Elevens, and MCC ground staff

Tom Adams played for Kent in the glorious days of Alfred Mynn, Nicholas Wanostrocht (Felix), E. G. Wenman, Fuller Pilch and W. R. Hillyer. An all-rounder like so many of his contemporaries, he was a punishing hitter but sometimes sacrificed his wicket through neglecting to play with a perfectly straight bat. Always very particular about the preparation of the pitch and the final use of a roller before play began, he showed a marked preference for going in first, when the turf was still in good order and the bowlers had not had time to settle into a consistent length. He used to gouge out a hole just behind the popping crease for his right foot in order to prevent himself from stepping out of his ground too rashly and being stumped – an irritating habit which annoyed both the other batsmen and the opposing bowlers.

An excellent fielder either close to the wicket or in the deep, he was also a useful change bowler. Round-armed and of medium pace, his method of bowling was unusual on two counts. Firstly, before beginning his approach to the wicket he always extended his right arm on a level with his eye, as though he were taking aim at the batsman. Secondly, on reaching the crease he bowled over – literally over – the wicket, a comparatively uncommon practice in those days when many of the round-arm bowlers preferred to deliver from round the wicket. His bowling lacked much guile but was straight, and on one occasion, playing as a 'Given Man' for the Royal Artillery against I Zingari (1849), he shared in the dismissal of *all* his opponents in *both* innings.

Adams was selected to represent the Players against the Gentlemen five times (1838–54), but achieved nothing out of the ordinary, his highest score being 23. He was a ground bowler at Lord's (1851–55) and assisted the All England Eleven between 1847 and 1857, making only rare appearances apart from one season. One of the original members of the rival United All England Eleven (see page 123), he played in most of their fixtures in 1853 and 1854 and occasionally as late as 1857. His service with Kent began in 1836 and lasted over twenty years, ending in 1858.

In 1845 Adams established the Bat and Ball Ground in his native town of Gravesend, but after three years he sold his interest in it. His favourite pastime outside of cricket was shooting, and being of a humorous disposition he used to tell many tall stories of his exploits with his gun. Slightly under six feet and weighing twelve stone, he was a good-looking man and rather vain about his appearance. Especially proud of his luxuriant growth of hair, he took infinite pains in training part of it into a glossy curl at each temple, known as a 'love lock' or 'kiss me quick'. He carefully preserved some of the tall top hats he wore in his playing days, and in his declining years he used one of them as a receptacle for his long clay pipes.

Arthur Haygarth, the compiler of *Scores and Biographies*, describes this portrait of Adams as 'a capital likeness'.

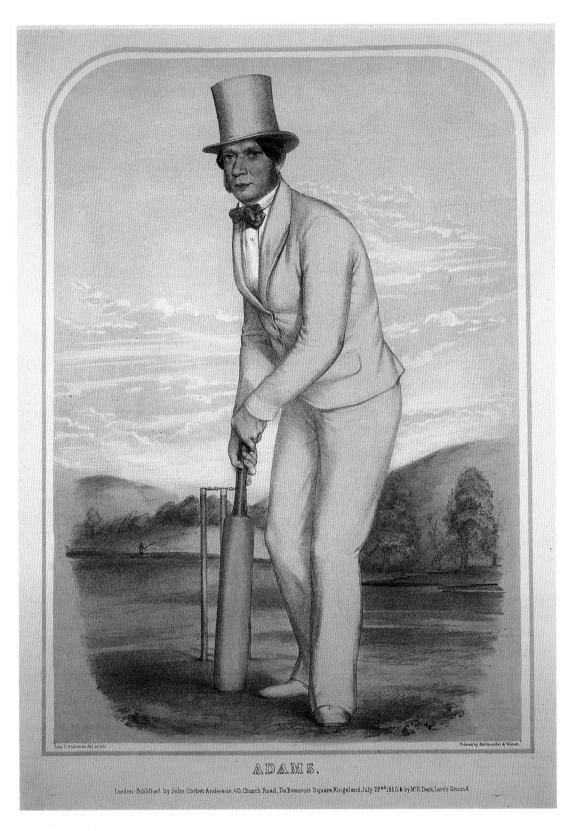

ADAMS.

London Published by John Corbet Anderson, 40, Church Road, De Beauvoir Square, Kingsland, July 22nd 1850, & by Mr R. Dark, Lord's Ground.

*Catalogue No. 5*

——— THOMAS BEAGLEY ———

Born 5 October 1789, died 21 February 1858

Hampshire

Tall and bulky, with a round-shouldered, stooping gait, Thomas Beagley is said to have borne a marked resemblance to Dr Samuel Johnson, the famous lexicographer. Seemingly rather clumsy and muscle-bound at first sight, he was endowed with a good eye and an abundance of physical strength, and was considered to be one of the very best professional cricketers of his era. He could take his turn as a change bowler if required, but his talents lay rather in the other departments of the game. His prowess was celebrated in a couplet from a contemporary poem:

> . . . worthy Beagley, who is quite at the top –
> With the bat he's first-rate, a brick wall at long-stop.

One of the greatest long-stops in the annals of the game, he saved countless runs and rarely muffed a catch. As a batsman he exploited his powerful physique to the uttermost and was particularly severe in punishing slow, under-hand bowling with scorching drives. On one occasion, rushing in to meet the ball at the pitch, he despatched it into the blue for a distance of 120 yards.

Beagley was still playing cricket in his fifties, certainly as late as 1844, but the details of all his performances on 'the tented field' have not been handed down to posterity. His days of splendour undoubtedly lay between 1819 and 1836, when he assisted the Players against the Gentlemen sixteen times, scoring 569 runs for an average of 28.45 – an excellent record in those days, when pitches were rough and unreliable and all hits had to be run out. His finest hour occurred at Lord's in 1821. After the Gentlemen had been summarily dismissed for 60, he batted at number seven and contributed 113 not out to the Players' total of 278 for 6, whereupon the crestfallen Gentlemen 'gave up', conceding the match. This was the first century scored in the series.

Cricket continued to fascinate Beagley after his retirement, and he was a familiar figure at Lord's. Unfortunately, he failed in his business as a builder and fell upon hard times. In an attempt to ease his distress, some well-wishers arranged a match for his benefit between the All England Eleven and Twenty-two of I Zingari at The Oval in July 1853. It was ruined by inclement weather and had to be played again later in the season. The proceeds provided some temporary relief, but poor Tom Beagley died in poverty, his exploits largely forgotten by the rising generation.

This portrait, executed in commemoration of the first benefit match, is 'an extremely good likeness', according to Haygarth. Beagley was one of the few subjects depicted in civilian costume by Anderson.

John C Anderson del. et lith.

Printed by R.Black Red.Lion Court Fleet Street.

## THOMAS BEAGLEY.

*THE ONCE CELEBRATED HAMPSHIRE CRICKETER.*

*For whom 22 of "I Zingari" and 11 of "All England" played a Match at the Oval, Kennington, on the 14th & 15th July 1853, as a mark of respect to merit, coupled with unassuming manner.*

*Catalogue No. 23*

# JOHN BICKLEY

Born 16 January 1819, died 15 November 1866

Nottinghamshire and All England Eleven

Slightly above medium height and weighing over twelve stone, John Bickley was a strong, stalwart, thickset man. An uninhibited hitter, he displayed no great skill as a batsman, but was an excellent fielder in the position of short slip, and above all a splendid bowler. Fast, round-armed, his approach looked innocuous enough to the uninitiated batsman since he took little in the way of a run, preferring to walk up to the crease. On arrival he delivered with an economical, swinging action, but the power residing in his right arm and broad shoulders made the ball bite the turf and rise with unbelievable speed, confounding many a complacent adversary. Every so often he produced an unplayable delivery, pitching just outside the leg-stump and breaking to the off with destructive pace.

Bickley played for the All England Eleven between 1849 and 1858, but apart from one full season in 1852 his appearances were rather infrequent, though on occasions he was engaged by the opposing teams as a 'Given Man'. Selected only three times to assist the Players against the Gentlemen (1853–55), he did little to justify a more regular place in the side. He was, however, regarded by his fellow professionals as a first-rate bowler, but he came before the public in first-class matches rather late in life. His opportunities for advancement were further limited by an engagement he held for several seasons as one of a group of bowlers employed by Lord Stamford at Enville Hall, Staffordshire. An enthusiastic patron of the game, Lord Stamford was not, however, always willing to grant his employees a temporary release from their duties to take part in important matches. Yet Bickley performed a few notable feats, the most famous occurring at Lord's on 9 July 1856. Playing for England against a combined team of Kent and Sussex on a pitch badly damaged by rain, he took eight wickets for 7 runs in the second innings, and all but one of his victims were clean bowled.

In his youth Bickley gained some local renown as a sprinter, but the burden of flesh eventually told against him in this pursuit. When not playing cricket he earned his living as a silk glove weaver, but later he gave up this employment for the more congenial occupation of innkeeper at Nottingham, where he ended his days.

Haygarth considers that this portrait is 'an extremely good likeness'.

*Catalogue No. 26*

# THOMAS BOX

Born 7 February 1808, died 12 July 1876

Sussex and All England Eleven

Thomas Box assisted his county for some thirty seasons and was a regular member of the All England Eleven for several years (1848–55). He was not much of a batsman at the beginning of his career, but by application and perseverance he improved beyond all measure, his favourite scoring stroke being a stylish cut. Although he was occasionally called upon to bowl as a change, he was first and foremost a wicket-keeper, one of the best professional stumpers in the country, and he formed a famous partnership with F. W. Lillywhite, the celebrated slow bowler also from Sussex. Box served his apprenticeship in those awesome days before pads and gloves came into general use, and he appears, in fact, without visible protective gear in W. H. Mason's well-known print 'The Cricket Match between Sussex and Kent at Brighton'.

Fair and handsome, his good looks were unfortunately impaired when a kicking delivery at Lord's hit him in the face and smashed his nose. This accident, perhaps, persuaded him to adopt a more upright stance behind the stumps, giving him a better sight of the ball. He had a good head of hair and, like Tom Adams of Kent, was very proud of it and wore it rather long, being exceedingly particular about its barbering.

A first choice for the Players against the Gentlemen for many years, Box appeared in twenty matches from 1834 to 1853. His record with the bat was moderate, but he rendered yeoman service at the wickets. Off the field he tried various forms of employment, such as dealer in cricketing gear, landlord of an inn, and lessee of the old Brunswick Cricket Ground at Brighton, but with only indifferent success. After the death of his wife he moved to London, failed again as an innkeeper, and found himself in straitened circumstances. He officiated as chairman of the Cricketers' Fund Friendly Society for a few years, but eventually managed to secure the appointment of attendant and ground-keeper at Prince's Cricket Ground, and it was there that Box, who suffered from heart disease, sadly but appropriately met his end. On the final day of a county fixture between Middlesex and Nottinghamshire, he suddenly collapsed after altering the score on the telegraph board. He died three hours later, and as a mark of respect the match was abandoned.

Box is one of the few cricketers wearing protective equipment in Anderson's portraits. The method of securing his leg-guards seems superior to the system used by George Chatterton (see page 71). These pads, reaching not far above the knee, resemble the 'shorty' pattern worn by some of the wicket-keepers in the 1980s.

Sketches at Lords N.º 8                                    John C Anderson del et lith

**BOX.**

Born at Ardingley Sussex, 1809. Height 5ft 7in.

London Published by John Corbet Anderson 40,Church Road de Beauvoir Square,Kingsland, March 1st 1857
and by F.Lillywhite,10,Princes Terrace,Caledonian Road,Islington.

*Catalogue No. 14a*

# CHARLES BROWN

Born 22 January 1815, died 28 September 1875

Nottinghamshire and All England Eleven

Charlie Brown was one of those useful individuals who could be employed in any capacity on the cricket field. As a batsman he evinced little appreciation of the science of defence, preferring a short, belligerent innings with the long handle to a prolonged occupation of the crease. He was primarily a wicket-keeper, renowned for the speed and safety with which he performed his duties. Like one of his near contemporaries, Tom Lockyer, an even greater custodian of the stumps, Brown was not averse to indulging in a little cheating or gamesmanship. According to rumour he would sometimes get rid of an obdurate batsman by surreptitiously tipping off a bail with one finger and claiming a dismissal. When called upon to quit his normal position at the wicket and bowl a few overs, he employed two actions, one a fairly orthodox round-arm, the other much more bizarre. An astonished batsman would suddenly find himself facing balls projected by Brown from *behind his back*, and he was at times successful with this extraordinary method of delivery. (He was also credited with performing this feat of dexterity as a 'party trick', extinguishing a candle with a small missile hurled across the breadth of a room.)

Brown never represented the Players against the Gentlemen, and had little association with the All England Eleven, appearing for them only five times between 1847 and 1857. He served as secretary to the Nottinghamshire CCC in the early 1850s. Restless, effervescent and excitable by nature, both on and off the field, he was widely known as 'Mad Charlie'. He was a dyer by trade, and in those days dyeing was carried out in one special area in a factory with all the craftsmen sitting in front of open tubs containing the different colours. Woe betide any unfortunate workman indiscreet enough to turn the conversation to cricket! 'Mad Charlie' became so excited that he would splash his own mixture into the adjacent tubs and completely ruin the work in hand, much to the annoyance of the foreman and his mates. Eventually, it is said, 'Mad Charlie' did so much damage that he lost his job and was compelled to set up his own business. Gods and mortals doubtless appreciated his choice of occupation: Charlie became a clothes cleaner!

This portrait was published by Brown himself. As can be seen, he was a tall and powerfully built man.

*Catalogue No. 17*

# JULIUS CAESAR

Born 25 March 1830, died 6 March 1878

Surrey, All England, and United South of England Elevens

A carpenter and joiner by trade, 'Julie' was not very tall but tough and sinewy and known for his skill as an amateur pugilist. As a batsman he had a strong defence, but he liked to force the pace with resounding on drives, cuts and leg-hits, and was one of the earliest exponents of the pull stroke. No place in the field was beyond his capabilities, though he was eminently successful at point and long-stop. A fast, round-arm bowler, his services were rarely employed in first-class matches, since nobody, other than Julie himself, had a very high opinion of his bowling.

Caesar first appeared for his county in 1849 and played his last match in 1867 – one of the periods when Surrey enjoyed supremacy in the world of cricket. He made his debut for the All England Eleven in 1851 and was not often absent from the ranks for almost a decade, finally surrendering his allegiance in 1864 to join the United South team. There were so many good professionals available in Julie's palmy days that he could not always command a place for the Players against the Gentlemen; he appeared in ten matches (1853–63), three at Lord's and seven on his home ground, The Oval. He was a member of two of the first three sides to tour abroad – Canada and the USA (1859) and Australia and New Zealand (1863–64).

Julie had an unfortunate experience in the United States, where some of the inhabitants at that time were still rather outspoken in their anti-British sentiments. Like his team-mates, he took infinite pains to avoid trouble by praising all things American and condemning all British institutions, as a safety measure. One night, however, he visited a bar selling one of his favourite brews, began to 'liquor up', and soon became embroiled in a quarrel with one of the local customers. Harsh words were exchanged, and Julie invited his adversary to come outside and settle the matter with a bout of fisticuffs. The American declined the honour, stepped back, and suddenly Julie found himself looking down the muzzle of a revolver. Concluding that the better part of valour was discretion, he succeeded in extricating himself from danger with some fast talking, made his exit from the bar and took to his heels, never stopping until he reached the safety of his hotel. He took a vow the next day that he would thrash the first American he encountered on British soil, even if it meant going to gaol. History has not recorded whether Julie ever satisfied this ambition.

A complex character, renowned among his team-mates for his constant flow of witticisms, Caesar was also a prey to pessimism and a nervousness of disposition that manifested itself in two ways. Occasional failures on the field he invariably interpreted as a sure sign that he would automatically be dropped from the Surrey team. Secondly, he had a morbid dread of fire, being convinced that any hotel in which he slept was liable to be burnt to the ground during the night. Julie suffered from the excruciating pains of gout in his feet, and this martyrdom undoubtedly shortened his career.

J.C. Anderson, del et lith.

Stannard & Dixon, Imp.

JULIUS CÆSAR,

BORN AT GODALMING SURREY, MARCH 25TH 1830.

Published by F. Lillywhite & Wisden, 2, New Coventry St, Leicester Square, London, June 24th 1858.

*Catalogue No. 34*

# WILLIAM CAFFYN

Born 2 February 1828, died 28 August 1919
Surrey, All England, and United All England Elevens

A sterling all-rounder, Billy Caffyn was worth his place in any team for either his batting or his bowling. One of the most attractive run-getters of his time, he was outstanding for the brilliance of his leg-hitting and, even more, the wristy elegance of his cutting behind point. His defence was good, but with appearing constantly on the true turf of The Oval he developed a slight defect in his technique by playing occasionally 'by guess', and he was never so successful on the rougher, more unpredictable pitches at Lord's. An excellent fielder any-where, he was also the finest medium-pacer of his generation. Delivering with an easy round-arm action he could bowl for long periods and was unaffected by weather conditions or the state of the ground. Playing for a combined team of Surrey and Sussex against England at The Oval in 1857, with 'the heat tremendous', he captured nine of the England wickets in their second innings at a cost of only 29 runs.

Caffyn played for Surrey from 1849 to 1863 and was extremely popular with the Oval crowd, who nicknamed him the 'Surrey Pet'. He made his first appearance for the All England Eleven in 1850 and turned out in almost all their matches in the next four seasons. Following a disagreement with William Clarke, the All England manager, he joined the United All England Eleven in 1855. Selected eighteen times to assist the Players against the Gentlemen (1850–63), he was only moderately successful with the bat and was not always called upon to bowl. As the only player to take part in all of the first three tours abroad – Canada and the USA (1859), Australia (1861–62), Australia and New Zealand (1863–64) – he holds a unique record. In 1864 he decided to remain down under, plying his original trade of hairdresser, and employed as a cricket coach at Melbourne and Sydney, making a contribution to the development of the game in Australia. Returning to England in 1871, he played a few more times for Surrey before retiring from first-class cricket.

Caffyn's reminiscences – one of the most valuable source books on cricket and the cricketers of his time – were published under the title of *Seventy-one Not Out* in 1899, when he still had many more years to live.

Haygarth declares this portrait to be 'an extremely good one'. Over the next few years Caffyn's appearance underwent slight changes. His whiskers increased in size, and by the time he paid his second visit to Australia a moustache had spread across his upper lip and a short beard encircled his face. Caffyn is also portrayed in the group of the United All England Eleven (see page 123).

John C. Anderson del et lith.    Printed by R. Black.

## CAFFYN.
Born at Reigate, Surrey, Feb.y 2.nd 1828.

Published by Lillywhite & Wisden, 2, New Coventry St. Leicester Sq. London.

*Catalogue No. 22*

# WILLIAM HENRY CALDECOURT

Born 28 September 1802, died 21 June 1857

MCC ground staff

A native of Blisworth in Northamptonshire and the son of a cricketer with a local reputation, 'Honest Will Caldecourt' moved to London early in life and became a ground boy at Lord's at the age of nine. Engaged as a practice bowler for the Marylebone Club in 1818, he retained this appointment for forty seasons until death terminated his service. As a batsman he paid little heed to defensive tactics, and though he was known to employ the cut on occasions, he was regarded principally as a 'hard slashing hitter'. In a minor match at Watford around 1830, he performed his most memorable feat with the bat: off successive deliveries he hit six sixes, smiting the ball out of the ground each time. Mr William Ward, a famous amateur cricketer and patron of the game, purchased the ball as a memento of the occasion, paying the price of two guineas.

An accurate, medium-pace bowler, Caldecourt clung to the under-arm delivery of his boyhood and could never be persuaded to adopt the round-arm action introduced during his lifetime. Though first-rate neither as a batsman nor a bowler, he was a superb fielder in his youth and was sometimes engaged in that capacity in single-wicket contests. He assisted the Players against the Gentlemen six times (1827–40), but achieved little of note. Caldecourt's activities were, in fact, most appreciated on the periphery of cricket – as a coach at Lord's, Harrow, Cambridge and elsewhere, and as a bat maker, selling his wares at a shop in St John's Wood, not far from Lord's. Above all he was an excellent umpire – his principal claim to renown – and his services were in constant demand in grand matches throughout many seasons. 'Honest Will' enjoyed a large measure of popularity, being a general favourite with both his fellow professionals and the gentlemen he coached.

Caldecourt is depicted in the garb he would have worn while standing in a match. Umpires at that time officiated in their everyday clothes, the familiar white coats not coming into general use for some twenty years and more. 'Honest Will' was a fairly tall, well-built man with a swarthy complexion, and Haygarth considers this portrait to be 'an extremely good likeness'.

*Catalogue No. 2*

# GEORGE CHATTERTON

Born 23 September 1821, died 1 October 1881

Yorkshire, All England and United All England Elevens, and MCC ground staff

There were few county matches in the north in George Chatterton's day, and he appeared only a handful of times for Yorkshire. He played intermittently for the All England Eleven (1848–52), but could scarcely be regarded as a regular member. Perhaps his relations with the team manager, William Clarke, were not of the best, since Chatterton was one of the group of professionals who signed a declaration which, in effect, established the United All England Eleven in opposition to the AEE. He turned out for the United as late as 1867, though only rarely after 1857. Employed on the ground staff at Lord's (1851–64), he was also one of the leading umpires of his time.

As a player Chatterton was a far more than competent all-rounder and a renowned single-wicket player at Sheffield, where he was born. A fine forcing batsman, he excelled at driving and hitting to leg, and he could bowl as a change, delivering slow, under-hand lobs with varying success. Above all he was a first-rate wicket-keeper, but had the misfortune to be playing at the same time as other famous stumpers such as Thomas Box and Thomas Lockyer, and often found himself fielding out while somebody else wore the gloves. He assisted the Players against the Gentlemen five times (1850–55), but apparently acted only rarely as wicket-keeper, since one or other of his two rivals was usually also in the team.

This portrait provides an interesting record of the protective gear worn by some of the cricketers around the middle of the nineteenth century. Chatterton's wicket-keeping gauntlets are, by modern standards, rather thin and devoid of much in the way of wadding. The pads, which are attached to the legs by separate pieces of tape or string, were rendered useless when these ties frayed or broke. This clumsy method of fastening, which is also illustrated in W. Bromley's painting of George Parr hanging in the Long Room at Lord's, was soon supplanted by the more convenient system of fixed straps and buckles probably shown in the portraits of Thomas Box (page 61) and Mr F. P. Miller (page 103).

George Chatterton and Henry Sampson (see page 116) were the only Yorkshire players to be included in Anderson's portraits of individual cricketers. This is 'an excellent likeness', according to Haygarth.

J.C.Anderson del et lith.  Printed by R.Black Red Lion Court Fleet Street.

CHATTERTON.

Catalogue No. 16c

# WILLIAM CLARKE

Born 24 December 1798, died 25 August 1856

Nottinghamshire, All England Eleven, and MCC ground staff

An expert player at the game of fives, William Clarke was partially blinded when a ball accidentally struck him in his right eye. This was a grievous handicap to his batting, but no impediment whatsoever to his bowling. One of the greatest of his type in the history of the game, he revived the under-arm delivery when round-arm was all the rage. Bowling from the level of the hip or slightly higher, and imparting considerable spin and break, his pace was generally slow yet full of variation without any change of action. A 'crafty and fox-headed cricketer', quick to weigh up his opponents' weaknesses, he was adept at exploiting a batsman's shortcomings and luring him into self-destruction. Playing for Nottinghamshire against Kent at Trent Bridge in 1845, he took nine wickets for only 29 runs (the tenth was run out) in the visitors' first innings, and captured seven more in the second (analysis not known). His only fault as a bowler was his notorious reluctance to surrender the ball to somebody else.

Clarke laid out the Trent Bridge ground in 1838 and came up to Lord's to join the ground staff in 1846. In the same year he founded his All England Eleven, the first and most famous of the itinerant teams. The AEE, of which he was manager, secretary and captain, became his principal concern throughout the remainder of his life. Under his guidance the team penetrated all areas of the country, playing against local sides and stimulating the growing interest in cricket. The AEE's existence was prolonged, lasting into the final quarter of the century, long after Clarke's death. The wily veteran was no philanthropist, but as shrewd a businessman as he was a bowler. His team was a financial speculation, aimed at putting money in the manager's pocket. At the same time, however, he unwittingly did good by stealth, as it were, by providing his employees with regular summer wages and making an immeasurable contribution to the development of cricket.

Caustic, autocratic by nature, and cross-grained – 'queer-tempered' in the idiom of the day – Clarke often quarrelled with his players, who found him overbearing and tight-fisted in money matters. Embittered by the treatment they had received some refused to play for him, and eventually his monopoly was destroyed by the foundation of the rival United All England Eleven in 1852. In spite of his business interests Clarke still found time to assist the Players against the Gentlemen ten times (1846–53), achieving a very good record with the ball. It was fitting that this hero of so many legendary feats with the 'leathern sphere' should take a wicket with the last delivery he ever bowled (All England Eleven *v* Twenty-two of Whitehaven, June 1856).

Clarke was above medium height and heavily built, and habitually wore a half-grim, half-smiling expression when things were going his way. According to Haygarth, this likeness is 'an exceedingly good one'.

*Catalogue No. 8*

# JAMES HENRY DARK

Born 24 May 1795, died 17 October 1871
MCC ground staff

An extremely secretive individual in certain matters, James Henry Dark was often unwilling to divulge information about his personal details, and it is even possible that his date of birth, as given above, is not entirely correct. From an early age until his retirement a few years before his death, his whole life was devoted to cricket. Regarded as one of the best umpires of his day, he was also a slow bowler, a forcing batsman and a fine fielder, though he made no particular reputation as a player and was selected only once to appear against the Gentlemen (1835). His far-reaching services to cricket followed entirely different lines, and he developed an astute business sense and a talent for administration that served him well after his playing days were over. Mindful of the welfare of professionals, he acted as the treasurer of the Cricketers' Fund Friendly Society and kept a watchful eye over its finances for several years. This, however, was but a minor benefit he conferred upon the game.

Dark, it is believed, first became associated with Lord's around 1804 or 1805 when, like 'Honest Will Caldecourt', he was engaged as a ground boy to field out during practice, thereby establishing a connection which lasted for about sixty years. According to the dates, he would have been employed on all three of Thomas Lord's grounds and may well have assisted Lord to transfer the famous turf from one place to another until it found its final resting place on the present site at St John's Wood.

Lord's was originally a leasehold property, and in 1835 Dark became the proprietor of the ground by buying the remainder of the lease from Mr William Ward, one of the leading gentlemen cricketers of the time, who had previously purchased it from Thomas Lord. Dark built a house for his residence near the south-west corner of the ground, established a workshop for the manufacture of bats and balls near the site of the present Mound Stand, found employment for several members of his family in different capacities, and undertook the management of the Club and Ground for some thirty years. So closely was he identified with the ground that it was often referred to in his lifetime as 'Dark's' instead of 'Lord's'. Deciding to retire in 1864, Dark sold the remainder of his lease to the Marylebone Club, who were subsequently able to acquire the freehold of the ground.

This portrait of Dark is termed 'a striking likeness' by Haygarth.

John C Anderson del et lith.

Printed by Kullmandel & Walton

Mʀ JAMES HENRY DARK.
PROPRIETOR OF LORD'S CRICKET GROUND.

*Catalogue No. 1*

# JAMES DEAN

Born 4 January 1816, died 25 December 1881

Sussex, All England, and United All England Elevens, and MCC ground staff

An ungainly, bucolic-looking man with a figure 'like a broad, half-filled sack', Jemmy Dean bore little resemblance to the beau ideal of a cricketer. Of only medium height, he had the misfortune to be cursed with an abundance of flesh, and all his attempts to control it were eventually doomed to failure. His good-natured smile, waddling gait and slightly comical appearance made him universally popular, and he was the recipient of various nicknames, such as 'Joyous Jemmy', 'The Ploughboy' and 'Dean Swift'. The last was not an allusion to any literary ambition, but a reference to his fast, round-arm bowling ('always straight and ripping'). Famous for his sustained accuracy, he had the knack of making the ball rise sharply off the pitch. Playing for MCC against Nottinghamshire at Trent Bridge in 1843, he took three wickets for 23 runs in the first innings and nine for 34 in the second. Increasing weight over the years inevitably brought a considerable reduction in his pace. As a batsman he had a high backlift and was regarded as safe rather than stylish. In the field he generally took the position of long-stop, where he 'would but seldom grant a bye', being for several seasons the most expert in the land. Sometimes, in the absence of a regular stumper, he alternated between bowling and keeping wicket – without pads or gloves – at the same end.

Dean assisted the Players against the Gentlemen eighteen times (1843–57), Lord's being the venue for most of the contests, and his position as a ground bowler (1837–61) may on occasions have ensured his selection for the team. One of the original members of the All England Eleven in 1846, he found William Clarke a harsh taskmaster and appeared in very few matches after 1848. In 1852 he was associated with John Wisden in establishing the United All England Eleven, for whom he played regularly up to 1857.

Advancing obesity finally brought an end to his active participation in the game he loved, and Jemmy became an umpire. On one occasion, it is said, he gave an unpopular decision and was pursued by a crowd of angry spectators as far as Lord's itself, where he was smuggled inside through the window of the Tavern in the nick of time. His protruding corporation prevented him from seeing his toes and, experiencing great difficulty in bending, he used to carry a special stick with clips fitted to the tip to enable him to gather up the fallen bails and replace them on the stumps.

Long after he had given up playing regularly, Jemmy took part in a single-wicket contest against a Sussex amateur of local repute called J. Pagden, whose gargantuan proportions (18 stone) made Jemmy (15 stone) look comparatively slim. The match came off on the Brunswick Ground at Hove on 17 August 1871. Pagden, it was agreed, but not his opponent, should be granted the services of a runner during his innings. Jemmy took the first knock, scoring 72 before allowing himself to be bowled, and then put the matter beyond any doubt by dismissing Pagden for 0 and 5.

A victim of chronic asthma and bronchitis, Jemmy Dean was found dead in his bed on Christmas morning 1881; one of the last to see him alive the previous evening had been his old friend John Wisden.

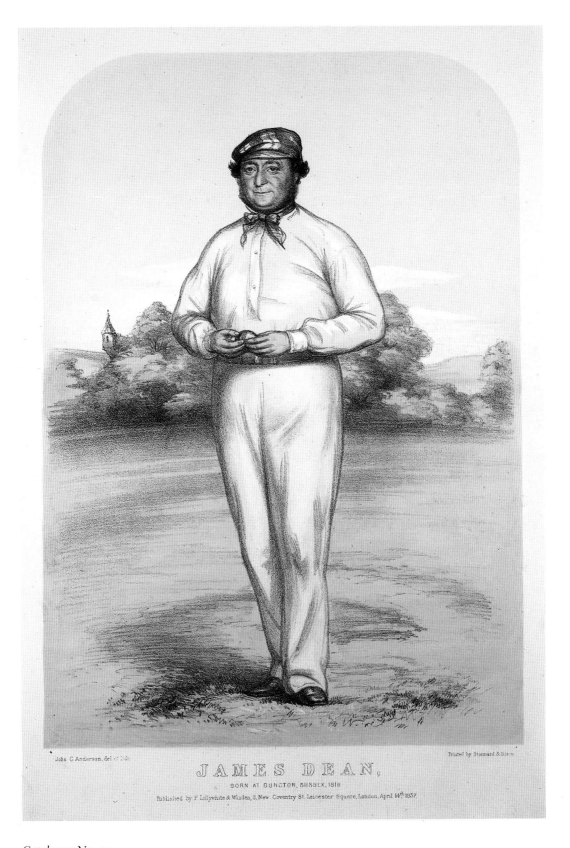

John C. Anderson, del et lith.

Printed by Stannard & Dixon.

JAMES DEAN,
BORN AT DUNCTON, SUSSEX, 1816.

Published by F. Lillywhite & Wisden, 2, New Coventry St. Leicester Square, London, April 14th 1857.

*Catalogue No. 31*

# ALFRED JOHN DAY DIVER

Born 6 July 1824, died 25 March 1876

Cambridgeshire, All England Eleven, and MCC ground staff

Originally apprenticed to a cook, 'Ducky' Diver soon gave up this occupation in favour of cricket. A small, compact figure with mutton-chop whiskers, he was proficient in all departments of the game, and his pleasant disposition and tactical acumen earned him the liking and respect of his team-mates. Bowling fast-medium with a round-arm action in his early days, he later took to slow, under-hand lobs as well. He was more famous as a batsman, possessing a strong defence and a neat, effective style which one censorious observer considered rather unjustly as too mechanical and devoid of any inspiration. In reply, Diver could have referred his critic to the record books containing details of his success as an opening batsman entrusted with the task of wearing down his opponents' bowling. An excellent long-stop in spite of his lack of inches, he often had to take the bounding deliveries of some of the fastest bowlers of his time, when the pace sometimes almost knocked him off his feet. Long-stopping gave him the opportunity to observe the accuracy of the bowling, and his captains used to rely on his advice as to the necessity of making a change.

Diver's career coincided with the brief period when his native county was considered first-class, but not all his cricket was played for Cambridgeshire. He held a brief appointment as a ground bowler at Lord's (1848–50), and he played for the All England Eleven in 1848 and was selected in all seasons from 1853 to 1862, though he was not ever present in the side. A member of the team that toured Canada and the USA in 1859, he also assisted the Players against the Gentlemen five times (1858–60), had many professional engagements over the years and was much in demand as a coach. Taking over from John Lillywhite at Rugby School in 1856, he retained this position until his sudden death in 1876. He was one of the most famous public-school coaches of the nineteenth century, being regarded as second only to H. H. Stephenson at Uppingham (see page 118). Diver was very popular with succeeding generations of Rugby boys, not only for his knowledge of cricket and his outstanding abilities as an instructor, but also for his civil demeanour and quiet, poker-faced wit.

Standing once as umpire in a match, he infuriated the non-striker by giving out his partner (the last man), when only two runs short of victory.

'I'll bet you half-a-crown you were wrong, Diver!' said the furious not-out batsman.

'Umpires can't bet, sir,' replied Ducky demurely, 'but' – pocketing the bails – 'now I'll bet you a sovereign, if you like.'

Diver's nephew, E. J. Diver, played for Surrey in the 1880s and later joined Warwickshire.

John C. Anderson, del et lith.

Printed by Stannard & Dixon.

# ALFRED DIVER.

BORN AT CAMBRIDGE, JULY 6TH 1824.

Published by Lillywhite & Wisden, 2, New Coventry St. Leicester Square, London, July, 18th 1858.

*Catalogue No. 35*

# GEORGE GRIFFITH

Born 20 December 1833, died 3 May 1879

Surrey, United All England Eleven, and United South of England Eleven

Stocky, short-necked, round-shouldered and 'tremendously strongly built', George Griffith was a left-handed all-rounder, and one of the best of his time. He could field anywhere, had an exceptionally long throw, and would deputize with the gloves behind the stumps at a pinch. His bowling was fast-medium with a certain amount of break, and in the early 1860s he added slow, under-hand lobs to his repertoire, often employing both styles successfully in the same match. For Surrey against Lancashire at The Oval in 1867, he took nine wickets for 130 runs, a remarkable analysis considering the visitors amassed a total of 429. As a batsman his defence was at first slightly suspect, but after several seasons he began to appreciate the virtues of playing straighter without affecting his hunger to force the pace. One of the hardest hitters of his day, he favoured enormous drives and leg-hits, despatching the ball out of sight. In a contest between Fourteen Gentlemen of Surrey and the Players in 1861, he lofted the ball clean out of The Oval. This feat was dwarfed three years later, when he encountered a first-class slow bowler in another minor match and smote every delivery of a four-ball over out of the ground for four successive sixes ('If George Griffith gets a loose one, he can send it far away.'). His most memorable performance with the willow in a first-class game occurred in the fixture between Sussex and Surrey at Hove in 1863, when he scored 89 in the first innings and 142 in the second.

A cheery, good-tempered man who enjoyed his cricket, a universal favourite and especially popular at The Oval, Griffith played for Surrey in one of her periods of glory and latterly, with the break-up of a mighty team, in her years of decline. A stalwart in the ranks of the United All England Eleven (1857–64) and the United South team in their early years, he also assisted the Players against the Gentlemen eleven times (1860–70), most of his appearances being at The Oval. Twice a tourist, he was a member of the first team to go to Australia (1861–62) and later was one of the party of professionals visiting Canada and the USA in 1868.

Griffith was often called 'Ben' or 'Old Ben' by his intimates, an appellation that clung to him from his school days. While on tour of Australia he received another nickname: the colonials were so impressed by his mighty deeds with the bat that they dubbed him 'The Lion' and 'The Lion Hitter'.

In the twilight of his first-class career Griffith suffered a severe sprain in his back while catching a ball at The Oval, and was unable to continue playing for Surrey. Subsequently he obtained several temporary appointments as a coach, and spent a short time as an innkeeper in Guildford. Suffering bouts of depression and a fit of temporary insanity, he died by his own hand at the age of forty-five.

John C. Anderson, del. et lith.

Stannard & Dixon, imp.

GEORGE GRIFFITH.

*Born at Ripley, Surrey, Dec^r 20^th 1833.*

Published by Fred Lillywhite, Kennington Oval.

*Catalogue No. 37*

# JAMES GRUNDY

Born 5 March 1824, died 24 November 1873

Nottinghamshire, All England, and United All England Elevens, and MCC ground staff

An automatic choice for representative matches throughout much of his career, Jemmy Grundy was acknowledged to be one of the leading all-rounders of the 1850s and 1860s. His favourite position in the field was cover slip, but he could acquit himself well wherever his captain placed him. He could also fill any place in the batting order, but often opened the innings in his prime, being a great sticker who surrendered his wicket with stern reluctance – except when battered repeatedly about the body by fast men exploiting rough, dangerous pitches. A fast, round-arm bowler in his youth, with a slight natural break-back from the off, he moderated his pace to fast-medium as he grew older, while still retaining his break. A fanatical apostle of accuracy, he aimed to pitch the ball a shade short of a length, and he usually preferred to beat the batsman unaided rather than bowling deliberately for catches.

His most notable performance occurred in a match between Nottinghamshire and Kent at Trent Bridge in 1864, when the visitors were dismissed for 62 in their first innings, with Grundy taking nine wickets and conceding only 19 runs. For several years his favourite headgear was a black velvet cap, which he customarily tucked into his belt when bowling, and he often used to keep a mental count of his analysis throughout an innings. He holds one unfortunate record – the first known dismissal of 'handled the ball' in an important match (MCC *v* Kent at Lord's, 1857).

A regular choice for the Players against the Gentlemen, Grundy was selected for nineteen matches (1851–68), achieving a good record with the ball. He appeared occasionally for the All England Eleven in 1851 and 1852, but found the conditions intolerable and willingly left William Clarke's team to join the United All England Eleven, for whom he played regularly from 1853 to 1865, and last in 1867. Appointed to the MCC ground staff in 1851, he served the Club for twenty-one seasons, being latterly the head bowler at Lord's. In 1859 he took part in the first ever tour abroad, to Canada and the USA. He did not enjoy the turbulent voyage home, nor his encounter at Liverpool with the customs officers, who were incensed by the boxes of cigars they discovered while searching his luggage.

Grundy's height was only 5 feet 6½ inches, but he looked taller because of his erect carriage, strong build and immaculate turn-out on the cricket field. Anderson's portrait shows him as a comparative stripling, but in later years he carried much more weight. According to one story, he was once standing as umpire in a match in the days before the officials wore white coats. Complaining that Jemmy's sombrely clad and, above all, ample bulk interfered with the sight of the ball, the striker requested him to alter his position behind the stumps. Jemmy duly obliged by standing sideways – but it made no difference!

J.C.Anderson del et lith.                    Printed by R.Black Fob[?]100 Grant Fleet Street

GRUNDY.

*Catalogue No. 16a*

# JOSEPH GUY

Born 30 July 1814, died 15 April 1873

Nottinghamshire and All England Eleven

Joseph Guy was one of the few professional 'cracks' of his time who was not a bowler; in fact, there is no record that he ever bowled at all, at least in first-class matches. A fine fielder at point, he could also take over the duties of wicket-keeper whenever the need arose. Later in his career he greatly distinguished himself as one of the safest and most reliable long-stops in England. As a batsman he was a model for all to observe, a forward player standing erect at the crease, unleashing an array of scoring strokes all round the wicket. Cuts, leg-hits and drives flowed from his bat, and he possessed one of the strongest and most stylish defences in the country. He was one of the original members of the All England Eleven, appearing in the inaugural match of 1846 and playing on a regular basis up to the end of 1854. William Clarke, the manager and captain, thought very highly of his team-mate and once delivered the following encomium: 'Joe Guy, sir; all ease and elegance, fit to play before Her Majesty in a drawing-room'. His technique brought him more success in eleven-a-side matches, since when the All England Eleven were contending against twenty-twos the presence of so many fielders inhibited his scoring.

For Guy, however, gracefulness reigned supreme, and he was particularly proud of his ability to defend his wicket with cultured style and elegance. This led some critics to assert that he deliberately sacrificed opportunities to score runs in order to display his powers of defence to the greatest advantage. He was, it must be admitted, too fast-footed to run in and administer peremptory punishment to the slow men. His detractors could not deny, however, that he was one of the most successful opponents of Alfred Mynn's fast bowling.

A regular member of the Players' team against the Gentlemen, appearing in all seventeen times between 1838 and 1852, Joe Guy achieved a batting average of almost 20 – high for those days, considering the quality of the pitches at Lord's. He never made a century in first-class matches – few batsmen did at that time – but for North *v* South at Leamington in 1850 he was unfortunately run out when he had notched 98, a mode of dismissal which he often suffered. It was some measure of his fame that the 1858 edition of *Lillywhite's Guide to Cricketers* should devote two pages to an appreciation of him and a detailed analysis of his record as a batsman.

Guy's occupation off the field was originally that of baker, but after he had hung up his bat he became an innkeeper in Nottingham. He was a well-knit man above medium height. Haygarth declares this portrait to be 'a capital one'.

JOSEPH GUY.

OF NOTTINGHAM.

London Published by John Corbet Anderson, 40 Church Road De Beauvoir Square, Kingsland, May 20th 1851, and by Mr R. Dark, Lords Ground.

*Catalogue No. 7*

# MR REGINALD HANKEY

Born 3 November 1832, died 25 August 1886

Oxford University and Surrey

Mr Reginald Hankey's career in first-class cricket was regrettably brief, lasting from only 1853 to 1860. He was educated at Harrow and Oxford University and soon came to prominence, acquiring an enviable reputation as one of the most promising amateur batsmen of his time. Aggressive even in defence and dominating the crease, he was renowned for the power of his drives and the majesty of his leg-hits. He was a good fielder at middle-wicket and a change bowler with an easy, controlled, round-arm action, but was inclined to be rather wayward in his command of line and length.

Hankey played once for Surrey, twice for Oxford in the Varsity Match, and five times for the Gentlemen against the Players at Lord's (1853–60). His fame in the annals of cricket rests almost entirely upon one historic innings in the fixture of 1857. The Players were in the ascendant in those days, before the best northern professionals declined invitations to take part in the series, and with the advent of W. G. Grace still in the future. In this particular match the Gentlemen soon lost both their opening batsmen to the destructive bowling of John Wisden and Edgar Willsher. Coming in at number four, Hankey was unfortunately feeling out of sorts and was evidently affected by the intense heat. Arriving at the crease, he said to those within earshot, 'I am far from well today, I shan't trouble you long!' Notwithstanding his forebodings, however, he began his innings by smiting Willsher for two fours. This early success acted like a tonic and, with his indisposition soon forgotten, he proceeded to flog the bowling to all corners of the field, completely mastering the awe-inspiring attack of Wisden, Willsher, Jackson and H. H. Stephenson, the medium pace of Caffyn, and the very slow lobs of George Parr. He was finally dismissed by a steepling catch in the deep after remaining at the wicket for an hour and three-quarters, scoring a chanceless 70 which included one six, several fives and very few singles, all hits having to be run out. The other batsman was Arthur Haygarth, the compiler of *Scores and Biographies* and a notoriously stubborn stonewaller, who made 20 during the partnership and was undefeated at the fall of the last wicket. When Hankey at last surrendered his wicket, little John Wisden heaved a deep sigh of relief, reportedly saying, 'If that's his form when he's ill, I'll be hanged if I ever want to play against him when he's well!' (Wisden's actual words, one can imagine, were probably expressed in a more colourful Anglo-Saxon vernacular.) This was Hankey's best score in first-class cricket. Had he been in the best of health and fit to run sharply between the wickets, it would probably have been even higher.

Reginald Hankey was six feet tall and possessed a robust physique, weighing nearly fourteen stone. Haygarth, most certainly an unimpeachable authority, declares this portrait to be 'an extremely good likeness'.

John C. Anderson del et lith.

Printed by Stannard & Dixon.

REGINALD HANKEY ESQ<sup>RE</sup>

London Published by Fred<sup>k</sup> Lillywhite and Wisden, N° 2, New Coventry Street, Leicester Square.

*Catalogue No. 27*

# THOMAS HEARNE

Born 4 September 1826, died 13 May 1900

Middlesex, United All England Eleven, United South of England Eleven, and MCC ground staff

One of the senior members of the numerous Hearne family – several of whom achieved fame on the cricket field – Old Tom Hearne was a native of Buckinghamshire but resided for most of his life in Ealing, where he kept a shop following the business of draper, tailor ('can make a cricketer a pair of flannel or any other trousers') and dealer in cricketing goods. A tall, spare man with an erect carriage, he was one of the safest and most reliable batsmen of his time, not particularly stylish but eminently sound in defence and always eager to go on the attack and despatch the ball to all parts of the ground. His wicket was one of the hardest to capture, even though he refused to puddle about the crease and liked to make his runs at a more lively rate than many of his contemporaries. Drives and leg-hits were his principal means of scoring, but he was fond of employing one favourite shot which had become obsolescent with the introduction of leg-guards – the old-fashioned draw, by which a ball pitching on the leg-stump was deflected at the last moment between the striker's rear leg and the wicket by a late, deft turn of the angled bat. Old Tom was one of the very last first-class cricketers to practise this hazardous stroke.

Hearne's fielding was as trustworthy as his batting. At home in any position, he was seen at his best at point, middle-wicket or long-stop, and he was also quite a good wicket-keeper. As a bowler he adopted a fast, under-hand delivery in his youth, but soon abandoned it in favour of the more common round-arm action. Straight and plain, his medium-pace bowling was often slightly short of a length, a characteristic developed from playing constantly on the helpful pitches at Lord's. He had a good eye and a sure aim. Assisting Middlesex against Nottinghamshire on the old county ground at Islington in 1866, he once stopped before the point of delivery, hurled the ball in the air, and brought down a pigeon flying overhead. This trophy Old Tom had stuffed as a souvenir of the occasion.

A protégé of the famous Walker brothers of Southgate, Hearne was persuaded to cast in his lot with Middlesex in 1859, and he was still turning out for his adopted county as late as 1875. Appointed to the MCC ground staff in 1861, he succeeded James Grundy as head bowler in 1872 and, surviving a serious illness in 1876 which terminated his first-class career, he retained his post at Lord's until he finally retired in 1897.

Hearne was a member of the first team to tour Australia (1861–62), the United All England Eleven (1858–64), and the United South of England Eleven (1865–76). He assisted the Players against the Gentlemen nine times (1863–69), achieving one of the highest batting averages of his time. His most famous innings occurred in the fixture at Lord's in 1866 when he made 122 not out, and one of his opponents (none other than W. G. Grace) recollected that Old Tom played 'his pet stroke – the draw – repeatedly and well'.

T. HEARNE,
BORN AT CHALFONT, St PETER'S, BUCKS, SEP. 4th 1826.

London, Published by F. Lillywhite, Kennington Oval 1859

*Catalogue No. 36*

# WILLIAM RICHARD HILLYER

Born 5 March 1813, died 8 January 1861

Kent, All England Eleven, and MCC ground staff

Billy Hillyer was a fair but rather inconsistent batsman and an excellent fielder, especially at short slip. Above all, he was one of the greatest bowlers of his generation and one of the mainstays of the famous Kent Eleven in the 1830s and 1840s. There was little aesthetically pleasing about his run-up: according to one observer, he 'shuffled up to the bowling crease like a waiter carrying a lot of hot plates and anxious to set them down'. His delivery was round-arm, easy and economical, making the ball curl in the air and break with venomous speed off the pitch, cutting right across the batsman and veering perilously to the off. The pace was usually around medium and sometimes above, but Hillyer evidently had little difficulty in producing a bewildering variety in one four-ball over. His contemporaries found it hard to classify him, since in 1840 he played for the Fast Bowlers against the Slow, and two years later for the Slow against the Fast.

His deeds with the 'leathern sphere' were legendary, but unfortunately the total magnitude of his achievements can never be fully appreciated because the bowling figures of many of the matches in which he participated have not been preserved. Playing for MCC against Oxford University at Oxford in 1847, he performed the signal feat of scoring 26 and 83 (his highest in important games) and taking thirteen wickets. This is the first known instance of a cricketer recording the all-rounder's 'match double' of a hundred runs and ten wickets in the same contest in first-class cricket.

Hillyer was engaged as a ground bowler at Lord's in 1844 and served as a member of the staff until 1849. He assisted the All England Eleven against teams of 'odds' (eighteen or twenty opponents) in the first three matches of 1846, taking fifty-six wickets! Apart from one season, he was a regular member of the side up to 1853. In addition, he was chosen to appear fifteen times for the Players against the Gentlemen (1838–51), usually bowling with devastating results to dismiss a total of seventy-one batsmen – an excellent strike rate, considering the presence of several team-mates equally expert with the ball.

Hillyer's physical constitution was never particularly strong, and he was a prey to frequent attacks of rheumatism, gout in the feet, and latterly more serious diseases, which undoubtedly shortened his playing career and led to his premature death.

When not playing cricket Hillyer followed the occupation of gamekeeper. A first-class marksman and an expert at his craft, he was frequently engaged to accompany parties of the gentry on a day's shooting. Often characterized as the 'best of all bowlers', Billy Hillyer was nicknamed 'Topper', perhaps on account of a predilection for wearing the type of hat he sports in this portrait, which, Haygarth observes, is 'an extremely good likeness'.

SKETCHES AT LORDS. Nº 3.

John C. Anderson del et lith.

Printed by Hullmandel & Walton.

HILLYER.

London Published by John Corbet Anderson, 40, Church Road, De Beauvoir Square, Kingsland, June 17th 1850 and by Mr R. Dark, Lord's Ground.

*Catalogue No. 3*

# — FREDERICK WILLIAM LILLYWHITE —

Born 13 June 1792, died 21 August 1854

Sussex, All England Eleven, and MCC ground staff

The patriarch of a famous cricketing family, 'Old' Lillywhite was a short, stout man with a benevolent expression, whose twin pleasures were outwitting opposing batsmen and smoking a pipe. Though of only moderate ability as a batsman, he was the 'Nonpareil Bowler' and without any doubt one of the greatest in the history of the game. A pioneer of round-arm bowling, he first came to notice in the 1820s, using methods that flagrantly infringed the existing laws by delivering the ball with the back of the hand uppermost and raising his arm to the level of the shoulder and sometimes even higher. His pace was on the slow side of medium, and he was a model of line and length, very rarely bowling a wide. Details of many of his achievements have not been recorded in full, but enough of them have survived to testify to the havoc he habitually wrought among his opponents. His appearances with the All England Eleven were sparse, since 'Old Lilly' was a difficult customer himself and probably did not get on well with William Clarke, the All England manager, who was notorious for his high-handed behaviour. In 1844 Lillywhite became involved in an acrimonious dispute with his landlord in Brighton and came up to Lord's, where he was engaged as a ground bowler, retaining this appointment until his death as a victim of an epidemic of cholera in 1854.

Old Lillywhite appeared in twenty-one matches between the Players and the Gentlemen, making his debut in 1829 and his exit in 1849 at the age of fifty-seven! On three occasions his services were temporarily transferred to the Gentlemen in order to strengthen their attack. His bowling record in the series was phenomenal. He captured at least 175 wickets – *at least*, and probably more by today's method of reckoning, since in several of the earlier matches the bowler was usually credited with dismissals on the scoresheet only when he hit the stumps. In the second fixture at Lord's in 1837, against sixteen Gentlemen, he took eight wickets in the first innings and ten in the second. At least two other bowlers were put on, and the Gentlemen scored only 108 runs off the bat.

Lillywhite's shortness of stature was counterbalanced by an excess of self-importance and a supreme belief in his own excellence, and some of his quaint quips have been treasured and handed down over the years. 'I bowls [rhyming with 'owls'] the best ball in England,' he maintained, 'and Mr Harenc the next.' His vision of an ideal game consisted of 'Me bowling, Pilch batting, and Box keeping wicket – that's cricket!' He had an unshakeable sense of his ability to dominate all batsmen ('I suppose if I was to think *every* ball, they wouldn't ever get a run'), and he scorned anything that smacked of inaccuracy ('Three balls out of four straight is what we calls *mediogrity*'). Old Lilly tended to regard himself purely as a sort of divine bowling machine. He was once highly aggrieved at being reprimanded by his captain for refusing to take a hot return catch, retorting in a hurt tone, 'Look here sir, when I've bowled the ball, *I've done with hur*, and I leaves hur to my field!'

Haygarth observes that there were several portraits of Old Lillywhite, 'some of them ridiculous likenesses' – but Anderson's work is the best.

John Corbet Anderson, del. et lith.    Published by F. Lillywhite & Wisden, 2, New Coventry St. Leicester Sq. London.    Printed by R. Slack.

## WILLIAM LILLYWHITE.

*BORN JUNE 28TH 1792.*

as he appeared at Lord's Ground on July 25th 1853.

*in the*

GRAND MATCH for his Benefit played between SUSSEX (with G. PARR) and ENGLAND.

This Plate is respectfully Presented to the Subscribers.

*Catalogue No. 24*

# LILLYWHITE AND SONS

## JAMES LILLYWHITE, SENIOR

Born 29 October 1825, died 24 November 1882
Sussex and Middlesex

The eldest of Old Lillywhite's sons to achieve prominence in the world of cricket, James was an average batsman and a medium-pace, round-arm bowler with a twisting delivery, whose career as a player was unfortunately cut short by an accident. Rather short and, for his height, quite heavily built, he was blind in one eye. A kind-hearted, good-tempered man, he was an excellent instructor, earning his living as the cricket coach at Cheltenham College from 1855 until his death. He was also the chief promoter of the Cheltenham Cricket Week. Founder of the well-known firm of James Lillywhite, Frowd and Co., dealers in sporting goods, he is probably best remembered for originating *James Lillywhite's Cricketers' Annual*, the famous 'Red Lilly', which appeared from 1872 to 1900. He was called 'Senior' to distinguish him from one of his cousins, James Lillywhite Junior, who was captain of England in the first two Test matches against Australia in 1877.

## FREDERICK LILLYWHITE

Born 23 July 1829, died 15 September 1866

Frederick Lillywhite made no mark as a player, yet was intimately connected with cricket throughout his short life. Solely as the publisher of so many of Anderson's lithographs he would have been remembered, but he made a vast contribution to the game in a variety of other ways. A meticulous scorer, one of the earliest and most zealous statisticians, and one of the first printers of scorecards (1848), he was also a journalist, serving for some time as a cricket reporter with *Bell's Life*, the chief sporting newspaper of the day. In addition, he was the original publicist of the first four volumes of that monumental work *Scores and Biographies*. Fred accompanied the team touring Canada and the USA in 1859, taking along for the production of scorecards his 'portable' printing press, an unwieldy piece of equipment that went missing once during its travels in North America. On his return, he wrote of the team's experiences – the first ever book about a cricket tour abroad. Last, but by no means least, he was the compiler and editor of *Lillywhite's Guide to Cricketers*, the renowned pocket-sized annual (1849–66).

A quarrelsome, tactless and outspoken man, Fred formed a partnership with John Wisden for the sale of cricketing goods, cigars and tobacco, but the association was ominously short-lived. Later he forfeited MCC's patronage of his *Guide* for publishing scurrilous comments about some of the professionals, mainly George Parr and Wisden, in the edition of 1865.

WILLIAM LILLYWHITE.
Born 1792 at Goodwood. – Sussex.

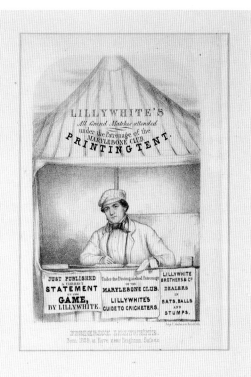

FREDERICK LILLYWHITE.
Born, 1829, at Hove near Brighton, Sussex.

JAMES LILLYWHITE.
Born 1825 at Hove near Brighton, Sussex.

JOHN LILLYWHITE.
Born 1826, at Hove near Brighton, Sussex.

*Catalogue No. 18    a b c d*

# JOHN LILLYWHITE

Born 10 November 1826, died 27 October 1874

Sussex, Middlesex, United All England Eleven, United South of England Eleven, and MCC
ground staff

The most accomplished cricketer of Old Lilly's progeny, John was a short, stocky, strongly built man who later grew a magnificent set of whiskers framing his face in a 'Newgate fringe'. He owed much of his success to the expert coaching he· had received in his youth from his father. Originally a very fast round-arm bowler, he reduced his pace after a few years. Revelling in wet pitches, he was known for a time as the 'Mud Bowler', but later he was rarely put on, even as a change. He was a good cover-point, but was famous primarily as a batsman, one of the best in England for several seasons. Vigorous and manly rather than elegant in style, he scored most of his runs with drives and cuts executed with all the power residing in his broad shoulders. Defective vision impaired the quality of his defence, rendering him eventually rather vulnerable to the fastest bowling. Even in his boyhood he had to wear spectacles for reading and writing, and he used to say wryly that he had also got many a 'pair' on the cricket field!

Unable, as were several others, to tolerate service under William Clarke in the All England Eleven, John found a more congenial billet by joining the rival United team in 1852, and he participated in most of their fixtures up to 1864, when he transferred his services to the United South, becoming the first treasurer of this new organization. Employed as an extra bowler at Lord's in 1856, he played for MCC in a number of first-class matches up to 1860. He assisted the Players against the Gentlemen eleven times (1851–60), achieving a good batting average, and in 1859 he took part in the tour of Canada and the USA. The proprietor of a thriving business in sporting goods in Euston Square, London, he was also the founder of *John Lillywhite's Cricketers' Companion*, the well-known 'Green Lilly' (1865–85), which absorbed brother Fred's *Guide* in 1867 and was itself later incorporated into brother James's *Annual* in 1886.

John was one of the principal characters in a famous incident which gave a marked impetus to the development of bowling from round-arm to the present over-arm. Standing as umpire in a match between Surrey and England at The Oval in 1862, he no-balled Edgar Willsher six times in succession for unfair bowling – an act which soon led to a change in the law, permitting bowlers to deliver above the level of the shoulder.

An excellent coach, popular and highly esteemed in the world of cricket, and always instantly recognizable on or off the field by his habit of wearing his hat or cap at a rakish angle, John was renowned for his good humour and pithy witticisms. Once, on being asked for his considered opinion of the notoriously bad conditions prevailing at Lord's in his lifetime, he was heard to observe with mock seriousness that the ground was not a billiard table, except as regards the 'pockets'!

JOHN C. Anderson del et lith.

Printed by Stannard & Dixon.

JOHN LILLYWHITE.

Born 1826, at Hove, near Brighton, Sussex.

London Published by Fredᵏ Lillywhite & Wisden Nᵒ 2, New Coventry Sᵗ Leicester Square and may be had of John Lillywhite, Caledonian Road, Islington.

*Catalogue No. 28*

# THOMAS LOCKYER

Born 1 November 1826, died 22 December 1869

Surrey, United All England Eleven, and United South of England Eleven

Tall and brawny, with a long reach and a good eye, Tom Lockyer was well above average as a powerful, hard-hitting batsman who was undaunted by fast bowling but notoriously nervous and insecure when facing the 'slows'. Himself an occasional bowler, round-arm medium-fast, his opportunities in this department of the game were few and far between, since Tom was for many years the premier wicket-keeper of his generation. Possessing exceptionally long arms, he was one of the first stumpers to take deliveries passing down the leg side instead of leaving them to the long-stop. Lurking like a feline predator behind the sticks, he gathered the ball with the speed of lightning, never neglecting a chance to stump or run out an opponent. He was up to all the dodges, narrowly watching the striker's movements at the wicket and perpetually alert for an opportunity to whip off the bails. Rumour maintained – and Tom was never at pains to deny it – that he had no qualms about persuading a naive batsman to leave the crease to do a little 'gardening', whereupon 'stumped Lockyer' was inscribed in the score-book. These questionable tactics were reserved for the occasions when the United Eleven were contending against 'odds'; at such a time, with twenty-two batsmen on the other side, Tom considered, 'We can't afford to be particular.'

Lockyer played only once for the All England Eleven in the early days, evidently unable to stomach service under William Clarke. He turned out for the United All England Eleven in the first season of 1852, missed very few matches up to 1859 and continued to appear up to 1864. In the autumn of that year he joined the United South of England Eleven, whom he assisted throughout 1865, with one match the following year. Chosen nineteen times for the Players against the Gentlemen (1854–66), Lockyer also took part in the tours of Canada and the USA in 1859, and Australia and New Zealand in 1863–64.

A skilled tactician and an excellent manager of matches, Lockyer was plucky and hard-working on the field and usually genial and companionable off it. There were times, however, when he appeared 'queer-tempered' and unsociable, though this arose largely out of a desire for a little peace and quiet and the opportunity to enjoy the soothing influence of a contemplative pipe. Once, overestimating the length of the luncheon interval, he finished his smoke but found on arriving back at the ground that he had lost the remainder of his innings. Another of his foibles was an irrepressible tendency to play to the gallery, with exaggerated stops and swift returns of the ball to the bowler. These ploys were exceptionally successful with the less critical crowds of North America and down under, who were unstinting in their praise.

Sweaters were not used in Tom Lockyer's day, and he was always instantly identifiable by the white flannel jackets he wore in cool weather. This portrait is 'a very good likeness', according to Haygarth.

John C.Anderson del et lith.                    Printed by Richard Black.

## LOCKYER.

London: Published by John Corbet Anderson 40.Church Road De Beauvoir Square Kingsland May 1st 1853 & F.Lillywhite 10,Princes Terrace, Caledonian Rd Islington.

*Catalogue No. 21*

# WILLIAM MARTINGELL

Born 20 August 1818, died 29 September 1897

Surrey, Kent, All England and United All England Elevens, and MCC ground staff

Billy Martingell worked at different times as a shoemaker and gamekeeper, but he chose to follow in his father's footsteps by becoming a cricketer. He migrated in his youth from his native Surrey to Kent, where he felt there were better opportunities to develop his talents. He learned the elements of batsmanship under the expert tuition of Fuller Pilch, and soon acquired the arts of defence. Being a natural forward player he was at his best against slow bowling, leaving his ground to meet the ball at the pitch. Though showing some early signs of promise, he lacked patience and, being rather limited in the range of his scoring strokes, eventually had to settle for a fairly low position in the batting order. He was a formidable bowler, fast-medium with a style all of his own. Like many of his contemporaries he went round the wicket at the extent of the crease, but his hand at the moment of releasing the ball was little higher than the hip rather than nearer the level of the shoulder. With such an action, bowling midway between under-hand and round-arm, he was able to impart more spin, sending down a fastish leg break. Impetuous and always eager to be attacking the batsman, he frequently ran over the crease and was notorious for the number of no-balls he delivered.

One of the original members of the All England Eleven, Martingell played in most of their matches from 1846 to 1852. Becoming disenchanted with the management and captaincy of William Clarke, he joined the newly formed United All England Eleven in 1853 and turned out for them occasionally up to 1858. He was engaged as a ground bowler at Lord's from 1856 to 1860 and assisted Kent and Surrey during the period of 1839–59. Selected thirteen times to represent the Players against the Gentlemen (1844–58), he recorded a good bowling average, distinguishing himself in the fixture of 1853 by claiming seven wickets for only 19 runs (six clean bowled) in his opponents' second innings. After his retirement from first-class cricket he was often called upon to stand as an umpire in a variety of matches, but he was principally employed as a coach at public schools, serving for many years at Eton. Universally known as 'Old Granny Martingell', he was popular with generations of boys for his expertise as an instructor and his quaint sense of humour, and it was a standing joke to hear him always refer affectionately to the ball as 'she'.

Billy Martingell was tall, fairly slender and lanky in his youth. Haygarth disapproves of this likeness on technical grounds. He insists that, in executing the portrait of Martingell, the artist 'has made a mistake in representing him with the two off guard, he defending his wicket with the two leg or middle as most other cricketers'.

**MARTINGELL.**

Born 20th August 1818 at Nutfield in Surrey.

London. Published by John Corbet Anderson, 40, Church Road, De Beauvoir Square Kingsland, July 8th 1850 and by Mr R. Dark Lord's Ground.

*Catalogue No. 4*

# MR F. P. MILLER

Born 29 July 1828, died 22 November 1875

Surrey and United All England Eleven

Short and burly of stature, Mr Frederick Peel Miller was a highly competent all-rounder and one of the most zealous amateur cricketers of his time, participating in countless matches from club to first-class level. Correct and stylish, with an excellent defence, he was one of the quickest run-getters in the game. The combination of superb eyesight and sturdy shoulders enabled him to hit the ball in all directions, but his favourite stroke was the off drive. He scored two centuries in his first-class career, curiously in successive matches in July 1860. A useful round-arm bowler of medium pace, changing occasionally to slow, under-hand lobs, he was also a brilliant fielder in the deep, with one of the safest pairs of hands in English cricket. His astonishing skill is celebrated in W. J. Prowse's valedictory poem on the death of Alfred Mynn, entitled 'In Memoriam' ('You may thunder cheers to Miller for a wondrous running catch').

Miller appeared twelve times for the Gentlemen against the Players, at both Lord's and The Oval, from 1855 to 1863, a period when the amateurs were weak and the professionals exceptionally strong. He also assisted the United All England Eleven occasionally, playing in their inaugural match in 1852 and serving as their president for a few seasons. A shrewd tactician and a superb leader always intent upon victory, he was captain of the triumphant Surrey side in the 1850s and early 1860s. He always paid close attention to the welfare of the professionals under his charge, and his popularity and the example of his infectious enthusiasm were an abiding inspiration to all the members of his team. Throughout his connection with Surrey he was one of the most influential figures at The Oval.

To the literature of cricket Miller also made a contribution. When Frederick Lillywhite, who had strong ties with The Oval, hesitated to publish the third and fourth volumes of *Scores and Biographies*, Miller generously offered to guarantee him against any financial loss. Subsequently, it is said, the guarantor committed a deed which has caused much chagrin to future generations of collectors and statisticians. Sales were disappointingly slow and, according to the story, Miller unfortunately succumbed to a sudden bout of anger and destroyed the stock of unsold copies – today, the rarest volumes in the whole series!

This portrait shows Miller ready to begin his innings, equipped with batting gloves and pads, the latter of a more practical pattern than those worn by George Chatterton (see page 71).

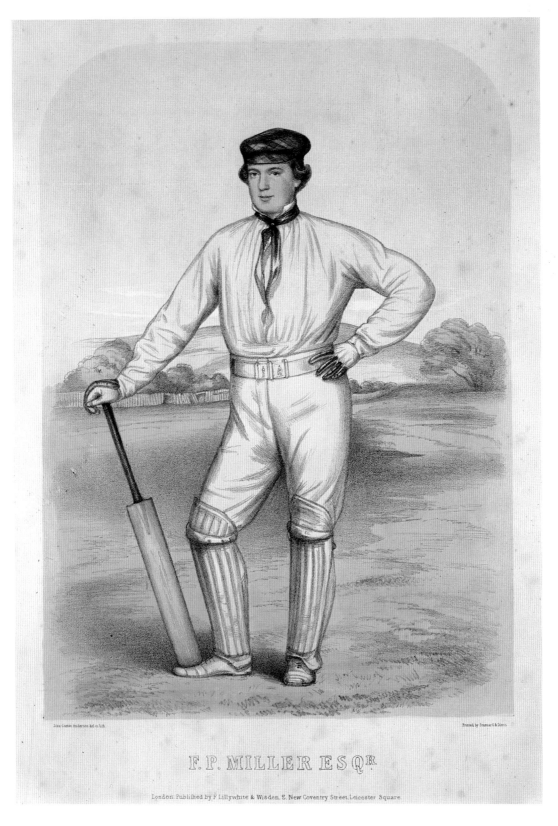

John Corbet Anderson del et lith.

Printed by Stannard & Dixon.

F. P. MILLER ESQR.

London Published by F Lillywhite & Wisden, 2, New Coventry Street, Leicester Square.

*Catalogue No. 29*

# WILLIAM MORTLOCK

Born 18 July 1832, died 23 January 1884

Surrey, United All England Eleven and United South of England Eleven

Billy Mortlock played for Surrey in the years when the county was represented by an almost invincible eleven of 'crack' performers. Always worth his place in the side, he was throughout his career one of the most reliable long-stops in England, sharing the first place with his contemporary 'Ducky' Diver (see page 78). Published statistics of byes conceded against the number of balls bowled in a season testify to his prowess in support of the wicket-keeper.

As a batsman Mortlock concentrated at the outset on mastering the elements of defence, and there were complaints that he sacrificed opportunities for run-getting, particularly on the off side, purely for the sake of survival. Cramped and awkward in style at this stage, and always taking middle stump as his guard, he was 'a pronounced crowder of the wicket', perpetually in danger of being dismissed lbw. On the advice of a friendly umpire he altered his block to leg-stump, and soon all criticisms were silenced as Mortlock blossomed into one of the finest batsmen of the day, combining his well-nigh unbowlable defence with a dazzling array of drives on both sides of the wicket and mighty leg-hits. At Lord's on one occasion he notched 7 off one 'mammoth' stroke (all run out), smashing the ball high over square-leg and through an open gateway into the road outside the ground. By 1864 he had acquired the nickname of 'Stonewall', or the 'Surrey Stonewall', a tribute to his impregnability as a batsman and a long-stop. Probably borrowed from the famous American general, 'Stonewall' Jackson, this was later changed to 'Old Stonewall', when Henry Jupp, a younger player of similar qualities ('Young Stonewall'), came into the Surrey team.

Mortlock was also a lob bowler, not one of the best but he was more than once successful with what was termed his 'slow, underhand rubbish'. Playing for Surrey against Kent at The Oval (1863), his bowling figures were 7 for 54 in the first innings and 6 for 73 in the second.

Mortlock turned out frequently for the United All England Eleven from 1854 until the end of the 1864 season. Then, like all the other southern professionals, he resigned his membership of the UAEE in order to join the United South team, whom he assisted for a few years. Selected in an emergency to fill up the Players' side in 1854, he made nine more appearances against the Gentlemen at Lord's and The Oval (1862–68), achieving a batting average of slightly over 25 – a very praiseworthy record for his time. He was a member of the first team to tour Australia, in 1861–62. Off the field he followed the occupation of dealer in cricketing goods, operating from a shop located near Waterloo Station.

Rather above medium height and with a physique bordering at times on the chubby side, Billy Mortlock was a cheerful, pleasant individual of equable temperament. His portrait also appears in the group of the United All England Eleven (see page 123), which Haygarth judges to be 'a pretty good likeness'.

W. MORTLOCK.

BORN AT KENNINGTON, JULY, 18TH 1832.

John C Anderson, del et lith                Printed by Standard & Dixon.

*Catalogue No. 38*

# ALFRED MYNN

Born 19 January 1807, died 1 November 1861

Kent and All England Eleven

One of the outstanding personalities in the whole history of cricket, Alfred Mynn was a man of superlatives. A massive figure, over six feet tall and weighing about twenty stone, he was the most accomplished and charismatic all-rounder of his time. As a batsman he was a punishing hitter, scoring most of his runs with doughty drives and enormous leg-hits. His bowling was fast, round-armed, delivered from round the wicket at a terrifying speed, and with an action that made the ball hum through the air on its way to the batsman. Mynn's style of batting and bowling was ideal for the game of single wicket; he was victorious in all the contests in which he was engaged, and was acknowledged as the 'Champion of England'. His stature and prowess earned him the nickname of 'Alfred the Great', and he was also sometimes affectionately called 'The Don'.

Centuries were very rare events throughout much of Alfred's career. He reached three figures once, scoring 125 not out for the South against the North at Leicester in 1836. This milestone was achieved at the cost of an injury that might have disabled him permanently, or even ended his life. Pads were not in use at this time, and Alfred received a cruel blow on the ankle while practising before the match began. Although he tried to rest on the first day and went in at number ten on the second, the activity aggravated his injury, and by the time he batted again his leg was badly swollen. Fearing, perhaps, that he might have to 'retire hurt', he attacked the bowling immediately, but during his long innings the sore leg was struck repeatedly by deliveries from Sam Redgate, a fearsome fast man. After Mynn had left the field, it was obvious that he needed urgent medical attention. A stage-coach was leaving for London, but Alfred's bulk and the nature of his injury prevented him from being accommodated inside the vehicle. Somehow his massive frame was hoisted on to the roof of the coach, and like a monstrous piece of luggage the wounded hero was transported to the capital. The surgeons intended at first to amputate the limb, but eventually decided on less drastic treatment. Alfred's leg was saved, and two years later he was playing cricket again.

Mynn assisted the Gentlemen against the Players twenty-one times (1832–52), achieving great success with the ball. Of farming stock, and ostensibly an amateur, he was an impecunious man, and it is certain that he received payments to play for the All England Eleven. The astute manager of the AEE (William Clarke) realized that the gentle giant would draw the crowds, and Mynn was a regular member of the team from 1846 to 1854.

Scorning such provender as tea and bread and butter, Alfred was a firm believer in a staple diet of beef and beer. The artist John Corbet Anderson recalled that one evening the sitting could not begin until the subject had consumed two and a half pounds of beef and a quart of beer. This meal was repeated two hours later, while breakfast the next morning consisted of a pound and a half of steak and once again, the 'inevitable' quart of beer.

John C. Anderson, del et lith.                                                Printed by Stannard & Dixon.

ALFRED MYNN ESQ<sup>R</sup>

Published by F. Lillywhite & Wisden, 2, New Coventry St. Leicester Square, London, Aug<sup>t</sup> 10<sup>th</sup> 1857

*Catalogue No. 32*

# THOMAS NIXON

Born 4 June 1815, died 20 July 1877

Nottinghamshire, United All England Eleven, and MCC ground staff

Slightly under six feet tall, with a spare, wiry frame, Thomas Nixon failed to rise to the top of his profession because he was deficient in all-round skills, being not much of a batsman and a rather mediocre fielder. All his craft lay in his bowling, which brought him many engagements with numerous clubs in different parts of the country, culminating in a permanent appointment in 1861 at Chelford, in Cheshire, where he remained until his death. He stood apart from most of his contemporaries of the round-arm period. Whereas many of them surrendered to the attractions of fast or fast-medium pace, Nixon preferred to cultivate the more subtle arts of slow bowling. Straight and accurate in length, he employed an action that made the ball twist and kick dangerously after its impact on the pitch. His greatest feat occurred when he was playing for MCC against Middlesex at Lord's in 1851. The full record has not been preserved, but Nixon succeeded in taking nine wickets in an innings.

Nixon's numerous professional engagements inevitably removed him from the scene of much first-class cricket, and he appeared only four times for the Players against the Gentlemen (1851–53). He recorded his best performance in the series in the second fixture at Lord's in 1851, when he accounted for three batsmen in the first innings and five in the second – again, no analysis was kept. From 1851 to 1857 he was a ground bowler at Lord's, as later was his son, T. H. Nixon ('Young Tom'). One of the fourteen professionals who signed the declaration connected with the establishment of the United All England Eleven in 1852, 'Old Tom' assisted this itinerant team occasionally up to 1856.

The possessor of a fertile brain, Nixon had some mechanical knowledge, derived perhaps from his original occupation in the trade of lace-making, and he exercised his ingenuity in inventing and improving various cricketing articles. Among his most important inventions were cork pads, which he first produced in 1841; open pads and bats with cane handles in 1853; the machinery for manufacturing the cane handles; and, about 1852, a practice bowling machine called the 'Ballista'.

J. C. Anderson del et lith.                    Printed by R. Black Red Lion Court Fleet Street.

NIXON.

*Catalogue No. 16d*

# GEORGE PARR

Born 22 May 1826, died 23 June 1891

Nottinghamshire and All England Eleven

George Parr was the natural successor to Fuller Pilch as the premier professional batsman of England, an honour which he held for many seasons until other rising 'cracks' threatened to supplant him. He adopted a crouching stance at the crease, which put his hands in jeopardy to rising balls but in no way cramped his style nor prevented him from scoring freely. Strong in defence, he was one of the first to appreciate the virtues of the hard block as a means of adding to his runs. In cutting and driving he excelled, but the leg-hit was his glory, and he was almost invariably cited as the model for this much-admired stroke. The direction was sometimes square, but more often behind the wicket. In Parr's day, it was considered bad form to hit straight balls to leg, and there were occasional murmurs that he was guilty of this offence. In denying this, one of his famous contemporaries admitted that 'he ran it very fine'. One of his most memorable innings took place in the match between Surrey and Nottinghamshire at The Oval in 1859. Though incapacitated with a damaged finger and a strain in his side, he kept up his end for over five hours, scoring a chanceless 130.

In his youth Parr was often stationed in the deep, having a long throw, but later he was usually to be found at point or short slip. As a change bowler he favoured high-tossed, under-hand lobs, delivered at a pace that made other slow bowlers look fast. Playing for the All England Eleven against Twenty-two of Boston in 1857, he took no less than twenty-three wickets in the match.

Parr assisted the Players (often as captain) against the Gentlemen twenty-two times (1846–65), and he made his first appearance for the All England Eleven in 1847, taking part in many of their matches for over twenty years. He succeeded William Clarke as secretary, manager and captain of the AEE at the end of 1856. An acknowledged leader, with some talent for administration – though he professed to dislike such duties – he was captain of Nottinghamshire and the teams that toured Canada and the USA (1859), and Australia and New Zealand (1863–64). Eccentric, blunt of speech and rather 'queer-tempered' like Clarke, Parr nevertheless inspired loyalty and devotion in his immediate associates. Beyond this circle, however, his character was not always regarded with such reverence, and he was believed to exercise too much influence over other northern professionals. In the early 1860s Parr displayed an open antipathy towards Surrey and the authorities at The Oval – in fact there were faults on both sides – and he was partly responsible for the growth of hostility that culminated in a schism between North and South in 1864.

Above medium height, with round shoulders and a slightly stooping gait, George Parr had a rosy complexion, auburn hair and the fashionable whiskers of the day, to which he later added a moustache. Haygarth declares this portrait to be 'a good likeness', but Parr detested it and replaced his copy in its frame with a coloured photograph depicting himself in cricketing costume without a hat!

John C. Anderson. del et lith.                    Stannard & Dixon, Imp.

GEORGE PARR.

Published by F. Lillywhite, of Lord's & Kennington Oval.

*Catalogue No. 39*

# FULLER PILCH

Born 17 March 1804, died 1 May 1870

Kent and All England Eleven

A six-footer of imposing appearance and build, Fuller Pilch was the most accomplished batsman of his time, renowned for the brilliance of his forward play. Adopting a comfortable, relaxed stance at the crease, he made full use of his height and abnormally long reach to smother the ball at the pitch. His defensive technique was practically flawless, especially against slow, turning deliveries, and even when merely stopping the ball he played with such a firmness of purpose that a quick single was often a possibility. He excelled at the drive, the leg-hit and the cut, and scored many runs by placing the ball just wide of cover-point's reach. A safe, reliable fielder, he was also in his youth a good, slow, round-arm bowler, and his all-round ability stood him in good stead in single-wicket matches. Later, he wisely chose to concentrate solely on his batting. His knowledge of the game was profound, and his skill in management of immense value to any side.

Born in Norfolk, and originally a tailor by occupation, Pilch accepted the offer of a salary of a hundred pounds a year – quite a handsome stipend in those days – to identify himself with Kent, and he took up his abode at Town Malling in 1835. Seven years later he moved to Canterbury, where he resided for most of the remainder of his life. One of the stars of the famous old Kent Eleven for many seasons (1836–54), he also appeared twenty-four times in the series Gentlemen v Players (1827–49), assisting the amateurs twice as a 'Given Man'. A member of the All England Eleven, he played in many of the early matches (1846–52), even though his career was then approaching its twilight stage.

Popular with his fellow cricketers and famous for his kindness to young players, Pilch was a quiet, even-tempered man. He was no conversationalist, though sometimes he could be persuaded to reminisce about the game to a favoured listener. Usually, however, he was perfectly content to sit back and let others do the talking, while he puffed away at a churchwarden pipe and took an occasional sip from a glass of what was ostensibly gin, but more often was just plain water. Throughout much of his career Fuller wore not a cap but a top hat, a fashion not without its distinct hazards for batsmen. Facing a fast, tearaway, round-arm bowler on a lively pitch in the first of two matches between Gentlemen and Players at Lord's in 1837, his mode of dismissal was, to say the least, unusual. The entry on the scoresheet reads: 'F. Pilch, hat knocked on wicket, bowled Bathurst, 9'. His Kent team-mate W. R. Hillyer (page 90) suffered a similar fate when playing for MCC against Oxford University in 1844.

Pilch was, perhaps, not the most ideal subject for artists. Without any specific reference to Anderson's work, Haygarth says that Fuller's 'portrait has often been taken, but none are very good likenesses'.

FULLER PILCH.

London Published by John Corbet Anderson, 40, Church Road De Beauvoir Square Kingsland, July 1st 1861 and by F. Lillywhite, 10 Jeaves' Terrace, Caledonian Road, Islington.

*Catalogue No. 10*

# HENRY ROYSTON

Born 12 August 1819, died 30 September 1873

Middlesex, United All England Eleven, and MCC ground staff

A native of Harrow-on-the-Hill, 'Cocky' Royston was a small, wiry individual of slender build. Initially a confectioner by trade, and in later years a tobacconist in London, his principal occupation was cricket. After some professional engagements he was appointed in 1843 as a ground bowler on the staff at Lord's, where he rendered loyal and devoted service to the Marylebone Club for many years. An all-rounder of not much more than average ability, he was usually regarded as a useful bits-and-pieces man. As a batsman he had his moments of success, though he had a fatal tendency to lose his wicket by holing out impatiently to long-leg. Keen and alert in the field – probably his greatest asset – he was also a competent slow-medium, round-arm bowler, once taking eight for 44 for MCC against Sussex at Lord's (1855).

Cocky Royston made a solitary appearance for the All England Eleven in 1848 and turned out for the United All England Eleven eight times (1853–56). He assisted the Players against the Gentlemen at Lord's in 1855, but achieved almost nothing as either a batsman or a bowler.

His principal claim to renown was as an umpire rather than as a player. Regularly appointed to stand in many matches, he officiated in no less than eight of the great contests between the All England and United All England Elevens at Lord's (1858–65). Rumour had it that his judgement in the matter of run-out decisions was not entirely impartial. According to one story, he gave out a famous batsman who had palpably gained his ground, later saying, 'I say, Squire, I was obliged to give you out, because we couldn't have won the match in the time if you had stayed in. We're obliged to study them things, you know, else 'ow are we going to win our matches?' Cocky as umpire was, one might say, as good as a twelfth man in a minor fixture.

Royston's most debatable decision occurred in a North v South contest at Canterbury in 1871, when he ruled that W. G. Grace was run out. This action was received with marked disfavour by the more rowdy elements of the crowd, particularly 'spectators located in remote spots not opposite the crease', and Royston was subjected to a prolonged bout of barracking. Unmoved, however, by this noisy, alcohol-induced demonstration from those who had paid their money to see W.G. make a long score, Cocky stuck to his guns, and the Champion had to go.

This portrait was published by Royston himself.

H. ROYSTON.

OF HARROW.

Catalogue No. 40

# HENRY SAMPSON

Born 3 March 1813, died 29 March 1885

Yorkshire and United All England Eleven

Harry Sampson – the correct spelling – was one of the earliest Yorkshire cricketers to earn fame in the Sheffield district, where he enjoyed considerable esteem. A sturdy, resolute batsman with plenty of grit and almost entirely a back player, he had a thorough mastery of the principles of defence and wielded the straightest of blades. His favourite attacking stroke was the cut, but he neglected no opportunity to score in front of the wicket. A good, safe fielder, especially in the position of long-stop, he was also no mean bowler. Though not often employed as a change in grand matches, he was sufficiently talented to be regarded as a formidable opponent at the single-wicket version of the game. His most famous contest took place at Sheffield in 1841, when he completely overwhelmed the legendary Tom Marsden – then past his best – by an innings and 50 runs.

As a northerner Harry Sampson was at a serious disadvantage in the matter of engagements to appear in important matches. Around 1841 he had a fleeting connection with the ground staff at Lord's, and the following year he became an innkeeper at Reading, but he played cricket only rarely in the south, where he was largely unknown. He assisted the North against the South a few times and appeared once for the Players against the Gentlemen (1841), being only the second Yorkshireman to be selected for the series, but much of his cricket was played in his native district. On very rare occasions he turned out for the All England Eleven, but in 1852 he chose to throw in his lot with the newly established United All England Eleven, though his name was not ever present in the team list. He once performed the extraordinary feat – usually regarded as a record – of scoring 162 runs in a match played on ice at Sheffield (1841). A popular and well-known personality in cricket circles in Sheffield, he was for some twenty years the landlord of the Adelphi Hotel, where many committees and groups often held their meetings.

Short of stature, Harry Sampson looked even shorter because of his bulk and heavy build. Haygarth considers this portrait to be 'a good likeness'. Sampson also appears – wearing a cap – in the group of the United All England team (see page 123).

*Note:* There could be a slight mystery about this lithograph. It is possible that Anderson might have intended to record the likeness of another cricketer then changed his mind and substituted Sampson. The original watercolour, preserved at Lord's and identified as Sampson, shows a man with younger, more handsome features, and the two small figures on the left are missing. *Cricket*, edited by Horace G. Hutchinson, contains a reproduction of the watercolour version, identifying the subject as Thomas Hunt, who appears in the print of the United All England Eleven (see page 123).

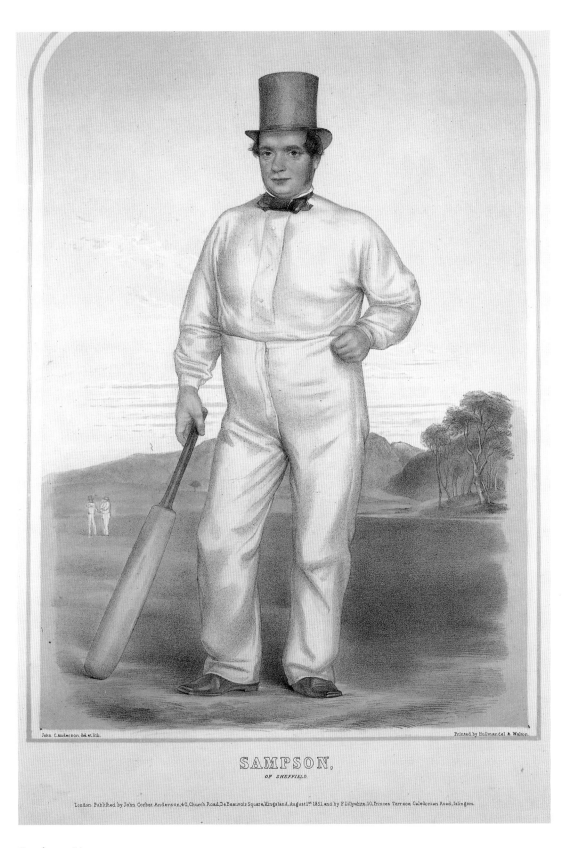

SAMPSON,
*OF SHEFFIELD.*

John C. Anderson, del. et lith.

Printed by Hullmandel & Walton.

London: Published by John Corbet Anderson, 40, Church Road, De Beauvoir Square, Kingsland, August 1st 1851, and by F. Lillywhite, 10, Princes Terrace, Caledonian Road, Islington.

*Catalogue No. 11*

# HEATHFIELD HARMAN
## ─── STEPHENSON ───
Born 3 May 1833, died 17 December 1896
Surrey, All England Eleven, and United South of England Eleven

Six feet tall, with a lithe, athletic frame, H. H. Stephenson was one of the most valuable members of the famous Surrey team of the 1850s and 1860s, and the perfect all-rounder for several seasons. At the top of the tree as a batsman, his defensive technique was sound and straight, but he was rarely content to sit on the splice and was the ideal performer for the occasion when the bowling had been collared. A punishing player, he was quick on his feet and made full use of his splendid physique to go on the attack. His favourite scoring strokes were powerful drives and full-blooded leg-hits, but he seldom employed the cut, being a shade weak in his off-side play. A fearsome fast bowler with a devastating break from the off – uncommon for a round-arm action – he was regarded as one of the earliest exponents of fast, break-back bowling. His success, unfortunately, brought on his decline: he was overworked, lost sensitivity in the tips of his fingers, and the erstwhile deadliness of his deliveries diminished. A good fielder and an excellent wicket-keeper, though his opportunities with the gloves for Surrey and the Players were restricted by the presence of Tom Lockyer, he was for years the regular stumper for the All England Eleven whom he assisted from 1854 to 1864, taking over the duties from Tom Box. He later joined the United South of England Eleven, playing occasionally from 1865 to 1875, but was never a full-time member of the side.

Stephenson assisted the Players against the Gentlemen fourteen times (1857–69), usually in the fixture at The Oval where, in 1864, he performed the then comparatively rare feat of scoring a century (117). His batting average in the series (between 19 and 20) was quite satisfactory by contemporary standards. He was a member of the party touring Canada and the USA (1859) and was appointed captain of the all-professional team visiting Australia in 1861–62. A widely respected man, he was socially superior to many of his team-mates, being in effect a 'gentleman' player, but his financial resources were too slender for him to play as an amateur. He was employed as a whipper-in and a huntsman for several years by the Duc d'Aumale, surrendering these duties when he was engaged as the coach at Uppingham School where he remained until his death, having trained and brought out many first-class cricketers. His fame in this role was widespread, surpassing even that of 'Ducky' Diver at Rugby.

Known universally as 'H.H.', he was sometimes referred to as 'Surrey' Stephenson in order to distinguish him from his namesake, Edwin 'Yorkshire' Stephenson, who was also a batsman/wicket-keeper, but no relation. 'H.H.' often wore a long black frock-coat reminiscent of the clergy, and George Parr nicknamed him 'Spurgeon' after a popular preacher of the time.

Haygarth judges this portrait to be 'a good likeness'. Stephenson's nephew was J. M. Read, the Surrey and England cricketer.

HEATHFIELD HARMAN
STEPHENSON,
BORN MAY 3RD 1833, AT ESHER, SURREY.

John C. Anderson, del. et lith.

Printed by Stannard & Dixon.

Published by F. Lillywhite & Wisden 2, New Coventry St. Leicester Square, London. March 12th 1858.

*Catalogue No. 33*

# THE SURREY CRICKETERS

From left to right: Thomas Sherman, Julius Caesar, William Caffyn, Thomas Lockyer

*Biographical notes for members of this group appear elsewhere, except for the following:*

## THOMAS SHERMAN

Born 1 December 1825, died 10 October 1911
Surrey and United All England Eleven

One of the longest-lived cricketers of his generation, Thomas Sherman came from a family well known for cricketing talent in the Mitcham district and throughout Surrey. His father James and his uncle John had both represented the Players against the Gentlemen three times (1819–21). Tom was above medium height and of average weight. His style as a batsman was acknowledged to be quite good and at times he made a reasonable score, but he was much too impatient to achieve any considerable success, often losing his wicket by leaving his ground and running in at the ball, and his average in first-class matches was very low. He was a good fielder, and his ambitions for recognition as the fastest round-arm bowler of his time were realized for several seasons. Always keeping a good length and aiming at the stumps, he tended to rely on the uneven ground to assist him in beating opposing batsmen. In his prime his bowling was considered so dangerous on rough pitches that William Clarke once objected to his presence as a 'Given Man' with a local side, declaring he would not permit the members of his All England team to be knocked about by Tom's expresses. Sherman inevitably lost some of his speed, and since he had little command of break or spin, his worth as a bowler declined.

Sherman was never selected to assist the Players against the Gentlemen. He had a reputation for being a rather difficult man to get on with, and eventually he fell out with the authorities at The Oval, though he returned to appear for Surrey as late as 1870, his first match being in 1847. The United All England Eleven enjoyed his services in several games from 1853 to 1856, but he was hardly to be reckoned as a regular member of the side. Tom Sherman was one of the founders of the New All England Eleven in 1859 and the New United South of England Eleven in 1875. The existence of both these teams was brief and undistinguished.

In a review of this print, *Bell's Life* commented to its readers that the four players were 'grouped in easy and graceful attitudes and are all lifelike in face and figure'.

SHERMAN.    JULIUS CÆSAR.    CAFFYN.    LOCKYER.

SKETCHES OF THE SURREY CRICKETERS.

*Catalogue No. 15*

# THE UNITED ALL ENGLAND
## ELEVEN

From left to right: *T. Hunt, *G. H. Wright, *T. M. Adams, W. Mortlock, *T. Lockyer,
*J. Wisden, F. Lillywhite (in tent), *John Lillywhite (on ground), *J. Dean, W. Caffyn,
*J. Grundy, W. Martingell, *T. Sherman, H. Sampson

Alienated by the treatment they had received from William Clarke while playing for the All England Eleven, John Wisden and his friend James Dean decided to form the United All England Eleven in 1852. This rival team consisted of those professionals who, like themselves, had quarrelled with Clarke, and others refusing to be associated with the All England Eleven. After an acrimonious confrontation with Clarke – the courageous veteran faced them *on his own* at Newmarket – the members of the United team published a manifesto declaring they would not play in any match under his management, apart from county fixtures. Nine of the signatories appear in this group (indicated above by an asterisk), and two others were George Chatterton (see page 70) and Tom Nixon (see page 108). The United's programme, like that of the AEE, was made up mainly of encounters with local teams fielding as many as twenty-two men, but after 'Old' Clarke's death the 'Two Elevens' played a series of benefit matches (1857–69), many of them rated as *the* event of the cricket season. The final game in 1869 marked the end of the United All England Eleven's existence. The team was never so efficiently managed as the All England Eleven.

*Biographical notes for all members of this group appear elsewhere, with the exception of the following:*

THOMAS HUNT, born 2 September 1819, died 11 September 1858. Yorkshire and UAEE.

Though a native of Chesterfield, Tom Hunt played most of his cricket in Sheffield and Manchester. Slightly above medium height and latterly rather portly, he was a splendid batsman, a fast, round-arm bowler, and an occasional wicket-keeper. Being a northerner, his appearances in first-class cricket were somewhat sporadic – he assisted the Players against the Gentlemen only once (1850) – but he scored 102 for the North against the South (Manchester, 1856), and he was an excellent single-wicket contestant, defeating several well-known opponents and earning the title of the 'Star of the North'. Hunt was fatally injured in a railway accident at Rochdale shortly after playing in a cricket match.

GEORGE HENRY WRIGHT, born 15 November 1822, died 28 November 1893. Yorkshire and UAEE.

Tall, well built, long in the arms and a skilful pugilist, Harry Wright was well known in Sheffield but, like Hunt and Sampson, rarely played in the south and appeared only once for the Players against the Gentlemen (1856). As a batsman he was basically a forward player, with a good defence and the ability to hit fiercely, especially to leg. He was an expert fielder at point and could send down a few overs at a pinch, though he was not often called upon to bowl. Wright was a familiar figure at Bramall Lane, Sheffield where he was employed as groundkeeper from 1866 until his death.

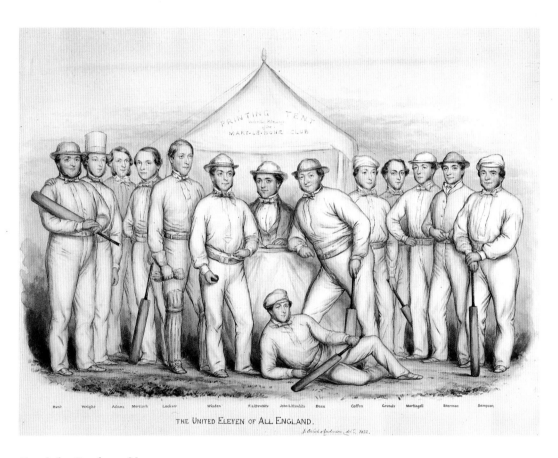

*Sketch for Catalogue No. 25*

# EDGAR WILLSHER

Born 22 November 1828, died 7 October 1885

Kent, All England Eleven, and United South of England Eleven

Ned Willsher was left-handed in all departments of the game and one of the premier all-rounders in England for several seasons. As a batsman he could hit as freely as anyone when he chose, but he was mainly a sticker with the dourest of defences. In his boyhood he mastered the arts of round-arm bowling in his father's orchard at Rolvenden, Kent, and went on to become one of the finest bowlers of his day. Straight, accurate, with considerable break from the leg, his easy, nonchalant approach to the crease was beguilingly deceptive: few bowlers produced a more deadly pace than Ned Willsher. He excelled at reducing a batsman to passive impotence and once sent down twenty-seven overs, of which twenty-six were maidens, for two runs and a wicket!

His action, however, was viewed with misgivings by some critics, who asserted that he broke the law by raising his arm above the level of the shoulder at, or immediately before, the moment of delivery. There were murmurings as early as 1857, but matters came to a head in 1862. Playing for England against Surrey at The Oval that year, he was first warned and then no-balled six times in succession by umpire John Lillywhite, and stormed off the field in a rage, only to apologize subsequently for his behaviour. Less than two years later the law was amended to make over-arm bowling legal.

Willsher appeared twenty-one times for the Players against the Gentlemen (1856–73), achieving highly satisfactory averages with both bat and ball. Joining the All England Eleven in 1854, he assisted them regularly up to the end of the 1864 season, apart from three years when professional engagements usually exerted a prior claim on his services. A founder member of the United South of England Eleven in the autumn of 1864, he was elected secretary and captain, holding these offices until 1872 when he was appointed to the post of captain of the bowlers at Prince's Ground, where he remained up to 1879. Strange to say, he took part in none of the first three tours abroad, but he was selected to captain the team visiting Canada and the USA in 1868. Nicknamed the 'Lion of Kent', he had a long and honourable career lasting well over twenty years.

This portrait shows Ned Willsher as a comparatively young man. He was quite tall and lanky, with a dark complexion, and various contemporaries described him as 'cadaverous-looking' and 'consumptive-looking', one even alleging that he had had only one lung since his boyhood – a strange claim, considering the length of time he played first-class cricket. Certainly his appearance changed considerably some years later, when he wore his hair cropped short and grew a beard, then bearing a distinct resemblance to Abraham Lincoln.

John C Anderson. del et lith.

Printed by Standard & Dixon.

EDGAR WILLSHER.

BORN AT ROLVENDEN, KENT, NOV⁵ 22ᴺᴰ 1828.

Published by F. Lillywhite & Wisden, 2, New Coventry St Leicester Square London, April 2ᴺᴰ 185⁵

*Catalogue No. 30*

# JOHN WISDEN

Born 5 September 1826, died 5 April 1884

Sussex, All England, and United All England Elevens

A small man with a whimsical expression, John Wisden tipped the scales at only seven stone at the beginning of his career. His lack of height and weight belied his talents. Regarded as one of the most formidable opponents at single wicket, he was an excellent all-rounder. He could field well in most positions, being particularly good at short slip. A patient, steady, reliable batsman, known as the 'pendulum player' from his habit of swinging his bat rhythmically backwards and forwards in a perfectly straight line, he scored many of his runs on the leg side and, like Thomas Hearne (see page 88), he was an expert at the old-fashioned draw stroke. Playing for Sussex against Yorkshire in the inaugural county match at Bramall Lane, Sheffield (August 1855), he made 148, his highest score in first-class cricket.

As a bowler Wisden delivered the ball with a perfectly fair round-arm action, never raising his hand above the level of his shoulder. Famous for his accuracy and command of pitch, his pace was remarkable for so small a man, being 'very fast indeed and ripping'. Even when his speed dropped to nearer medium he remained a dangerous adversary, and towards the end of his career he took to bowling under-arm lobs as well with considerable success. In 1849 he became joint proprietor (with George Parr) of a cricket ground at Leamington, acquiring a somewhat tenuous qualification to play for the North against the South, and in the match at Lord's in 1850 he performed the astonishing feat of clean bowling all ten wickets in the South's second innings with a lethal spell of fast off breaks and shooters (analysis, alas, not known).

Wisden represented the Players against the Gentlemen fifteen times (1848–59), achieving a good record as batsman and bowler, and he first appeared for the All England Eleven in 1847. Normally an easy-going man, he found himself unable to maintain a pleasant relationship with the cantankerous William Clarke, and with the assistance of James Dean he founded the rival United All England Eleven in 1852. He was a member, and one of the guiding lights, of the team that toured Canada and the USA in 1859.

In 1855 Wisden formed a partnership with Fred Lillywhite to set up a 'cricketing and cigar depot' near Leicester Square, London, and remained in business on his own from 1858 onwards, conducting a successful enterprise. He retired from active cricket in 1863, a year before the first appearance of his famous *Almanack*, the 'cricketer's bible'.

Wisden was nicknamed the 'Little Wonder', and sometimes 'The Cardinal'. In both the large and small versions of Anderson's portrait he is sporting a cap, but he is credited with being the first eminent player to assume a straw hat on the cricket field, and he is, perhaps, wearing this headgear in the group of the United All England Eleven (see page 123). In later years he became rather stout, and his whimsical expression was partly concealed by a dark, bushy beard.

John C. Anderson del et lith.

Printed by Richard Black.

## WISDEN.
Born at Brighton.

London. Published by John Corbet Anderson 40, Church Road, De Beauvoir Square Kingsland April 1st 1852, and by F. Lillywhite, 10. Princes Terrace Caledonian Rd. Islington.

*Catalogue No. 19*

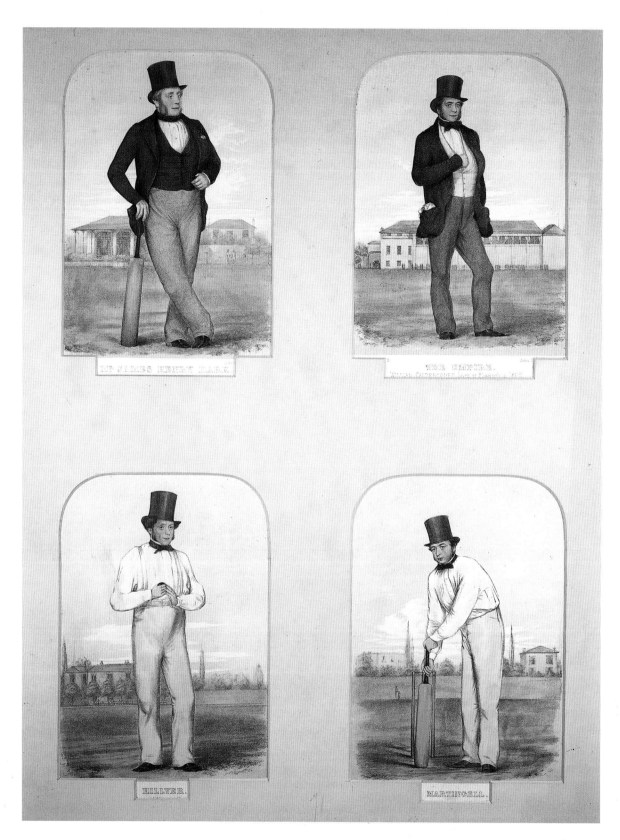

*Catalogue No. 12   a b c d*

*Catalogue No. 13 a b c d*

Sketches at Lord's Nᵒ 5.                                    John C Anderson Sculpt. lith.

**BOX.**

Born at Ardingley Sussex 1809 Height 5ft 7in.

London Published by John Cother Anderson, 46 Church Road, de Bennetor Square, England, March 1ˢᵗ 1852.
and by J.W.Lydeles, 20 Panton Charism Cross Ross Islington.

Sketches at Lord's Nᵒ 10.                                 John C Anderson del. et lith.

**GEORGE PARR.**

Born at Radcliff near Nottingham, 1826 Height 5 ft 9 in.

London Published by John Cother Anderson 46 Church Road de Bennetor Square England, March 1ˢᵗ 1852.
et by J.Lydeshire, 20 Panton Bennetor Charism Cross Islington.

Sketches at Lord's Nᵒ 11.                                 John C Anderson del. et lith.

**JOSEPH GUY.**

Born at Nottingham in 1814 Height 5ft 9in.

London Published at John Cother Anderson 46 Church Road de Bennetor Sq England March 1ˢᵗ 1852.
and by J.W.Lydeshire 20 Panton Charism Cross Road Islington.

Sketches at Lord's Nᵒ 2.                                  John C Anderson del et lith.

**CLARKE.**

Slow Bowler of Nottingham, Secretary to the All England Eleven

London Published by John Cother Anderson 46 Church Road de Bennetor Square England, March 1ˢᵗ 1852, and by
J.W.Lydeshire 20 Panton Charism Cross Road Islington.

*Catalogue No. 14   a b c d*

GRUNDY.

CHATTERTON.

DEAN.

NIXON.

*Catalogue No. 16   a b c d*

John C. Anderson, del. et lith.                                                    Stannard & Dixon.

STANDING IN ATTITUDE.
Nº 1.

Catalogue No. 41

John C. Anderson, del et lith.

Stannard & Dixon

# THE DRAW.

Nº 2.

London, Published May, 1ˢᵗ 1860 by F Lillywhite, Kennington Oval.

*Catalogue No. 42*

John C. Anderson, del et lith.

# THE CUT.

Nº 3.

London, Published May, 1st 1860, by F. Lillywhite, Kennington Oval.

*Catalogue No. 43*

John C Anderson, del et lith.

Stannard & Dixon

LEG HIT.

Nº 4.

London, Published May, 1st 1860, by F. Lillywhite, Kennington Oval.

*Catalogue No. 44*

John C Anderson, del. et lith.

Stannard & Dixon

FORWARD PLAY.

Nº 5.

London, Published May, 1ˢᵗ 1860 by F Lilliwhite, Kennington Oval.

*Catalogue No. 45*

John C. Anderson, del. et lith.                    Stannard & Dixon.

## BACK PLAY.

Nº 6.

London, Published May, 1ˢᵗ 1860, by F. Lillhwhite, Kennington Oval.

*Catalogue No. 46*

John C. Anderson, del et lith.

Stannard & Dixon.

## THE BOWLER.

Nº 7.

London, Published May, 1ˢᵗ 1860, by F. Lillywhite, Kennington Oval.

*Catalogue No. 47*

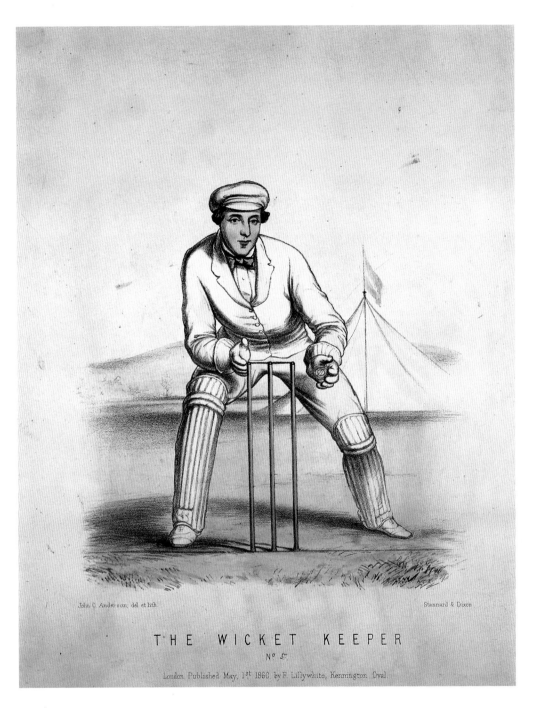

John C. Anderson, del et lith.                                                                 Stannard & Dixon

THE WICKET KEEPER

Nº 5.

London, Published May, 1st 1860, by F. Lillywhite, Kennington Oval.

*Catalogue No. 48*

# Bibliography

## Anderson's
## Written Works
*(in chronological order of publication)*

*Monuments and Antiquities of Croydon Church* (J. C. Anderson, Croydon, 1855)

Traveller, *To India and Back by the Cape* (1859). Drawings by J.C.A.

*Shropshire: Its Early History and Antiquities* (Willis and Southeran, London, 1864)

*Antiquities of Croydon Church, Destroyed by Fire 5th January 1867* (J. R. Smith, London, 1867)

*The Roman City of Uriconium at Wroxeter, Salop* (J. R. Smith, London, 1867)

J. Nash, *The Mansions of England*. J.C.A. drew all the illustrations for the 1869 edition

*Croydon Church, Past and Present* (Wertheimer, Lea and Co., London, 1871)

W. H. Rule and J. C. Anderson, *Biblical Monuments* (1871). J.C.A. was responsible for the illustrations

*The Chronicles of the Parish of Croydon* – in four parts:
  i) 'Prehistoric and Roman Croydon' (1874)
  ii) 'Saxon Croydon' (1877)
  iii) 'Parish Church and Register' – Whitgift Hospital (1878)
  iv) 'Croydon Archiepiscopal Palace' – Biographical (1879)

These four parts were revised and extended later to appear in one volume.

C. Bridger, *The Family of Leete* (1881). Edited by J.C.A. after the death of Bridger

*A Short Chronicle Concerning the Parish of Croydon* (London, 1882).

*Old Testament and Monumental Coincidences, with an historical essay on Christianity and its early introduction into Britain* (G. Bell and Sons, London, 1895)

*The Great North Wood; with a Geological, Topographical and Historical Description of Upper, West and South Norwood in the County of Surrey* (Privately printed, 1898)

J. Leete, *The Family of Leete* (1906). Almost solely the work of J.C.A.

# *Further Reading*

The main sources used during this book's preparation are listed below:

*Cricket Scores and Biographies*, 15 vols
*The Guide to Cricketers*, ed. Frederick Lillywhite
*James Lillywhite's Cricketers' Annual*
*John Lillywhite's Cricketers' Companion* (later *John & James . . .* and finally *James Lillywhite's Cricketers' Companion*)
*John Wisden's Cricketers' Almanack*
*Baily's Magazine of Sports and Pastimes*
*Cricket: A Weekly Record of the Game*
*The Cricketer*

Alverstone, The Rt Hon. Lord, and C. W. Alcock (eds), *Surrey Cricket: Its History and Associations* (London: Longmans, Green and Co., 1904)

Arlott, John (comp.), *From Hambledon to Lord's: The Classics of Cricket* (London: Christopher Johnson Publishers Ltd, 1948)

Arlott, John (comp.), *The Middle Ages of Cricket* (London: Christopher Johnson, n.d. [1949])

Arlott, John, *The Picture of Cricket* (London: Penguin Books, 1955)

Ashley-Cooper, F. S., *Nottinghamshire Cricket and Cricketers* (Nottingham: Henry B. Saxton, n.d. [1923])

Bailey, Philip, Philip Thorn, and Peter Wynne-Thomas, *Who's Who of Cricketers* (Feltham: Newnes Books, 1984)

Bettesworth, W. A., *The Walkers of Southgate: A Famous Brotherhood of Cricketers*, ed. by E. T. Sachs (London: Methuen & Co., 1900)

Bettesworth, W. A., *Chats on the Cricket Field*, with Explanatory Notes by F. S. Ashley-Cooper (London: Merritt & Hatcher Ltd, n.d. [1910])

Brodribb, Gerald, *Felix on the Bat: being a Memoir of Nicholas Felix* (London: Eyre & Spottiswoode, 1962)

Caffyn, William, *see* 'Mid-on'

Cardus, N. and Arlott, J. *The Noblest Game* (London, Harrap, 1969)

Daft, Richard, *Kings of Cricket* (Bristol: J. W. Arrowsmith; London: Simpkin, Marshall, Hamilton, Kent & Company Ltd, n.d. [1893])

Daft, Richard, *A Cricketer's Yarns*, ed., with an Introduction, by F. S. Ashley-Cooper (London: Chapman and Hall Ltd, 1926)

Gale, Frederick, *Echoes from Old Cricket Fields* (London: Simpkin, Marshall and Co., 1871; rpt Wakefield: S.R. Publishers Ltd, 1972)

Gale, Frederick, *The Game of Cricket*, 2nd ed. (London: Swan Sonnenschein & Co., 1888)

Harris, The Rt Hon. Lord, *The History of Kent County Cricket* (London: Eyre & Spottiswoode, 1907)

Lillywhite, Fred., *The English Cricketers' Trip to Canada and the United States* (London: F. Lillywhite, Kent & Co., 1860; rpt, Introduction by Robin Marlar, Tadworth, Surrey: World's Work Ltd, 1980)

'Mid-on', R. P. Daft (ed.), *Seventy-one Not Out: The Reminiscences of William Caffyn* (Edinburgh and London: William Blackwood and Sons, 1899)

Montgomery, H. H., *Old Cricket and Cricketers* (London: H. Stacey Gold; Wright & Co., n.d. [1890])

Morrah, Patrick, *Alfred Mynn and the Cricketers of His Time* (London: Eyre & Spottiswoode, 1963)

Pullin, A. W. ('Old Ebor'), *Talks with Old English Cricketers* (Edinburgh and London: William Blackwood and Sons, 1900)

Pycroft, The Rev. James, *The Cricket-field, with Some Notes by H. H. Stephenson*, ed., with an Introduction, by F. S. Ashley-Cooper (London: St James's Press Co. Ltd, 1922)

Pycroft, The Rev. James, *Cricketana* (London: Longman, Green, Longman, Roberts & Green, 1865)

Taylor, Alfred D., *Sussex Cricket in the Olden Time, with Glances at the Present* (Hove: Hove Printing and Publishing Company Ltd, n.d. [1900])

Taylor, Alfred D., *The Story of a Cricket Picture (Sussex and Kent)* (Hove: Emery & Son Ltd, 1923)

Thomas, Peter, *Yorkshire Cricketers 1839–1939* (Manchester: Derek Hodgson Publisher, 1973)

Warner, Sir Pelham, *Gentlemen v. Players 1806–1949* (London: George G. Harrap & Co. Ltd, 1950)

West, G. Derek, *The Elevens of England* (London: Darf Publishers Ltd, 1988)

Wynne-Thomas, Peter, *Nottinghamshire Cricketers 1821–1914* (Haughton, Retford, Notts: The Author, 1971)

# Index

Page references in **bold** refer to a player's biography and in *italic* to illustrations.